The Way to Great Freedom

THERE
IS
NO
SELF

MUWI HAEGONG

poppypub

나는 없다 THERE IS NO SELF
Copyright © 2007 by Muwi Haegong
All rights reserved.

First published in Korea in 2007 by Chaeksesang.
English translation rights arranged with the author.
Translation copyright © 2022 by Gagil

No part of this publication may be reproduced, stored or transmitted in any form or by any means, electronic, mechanical, photocopying, recording, scanning, or otherwise without written permission from the publisher. It is illegal to copy this book, post it to a website, or distribute it by any other means without permission.

Translated by Gagil
Published by POPPYPUB, Fort Lee www.poppypub.com
poppypub is a trademark of POPPYPUB LLC.

ISBN 978-1-952787-22-5 (paperback)
ISBN 978-1-952787-23-2 (ebook)

there is no samsara (eternal cycle of rebirth)

there is no heaven and hell

there is no world after death

all these are

no more than delusions

Preface

Among seven billion human beings, not one person doesn't wish for a happy life and to be free, with no obstacles, to be able to cast aside all the restraints that are put upon our lives.

But what is the reality? Far from being free, as the years go by, as wealth and power become more important to us, we sink into a deep pit, moving further away from a free and happy life.

Our minds deteriorate and our bodies become ill. The people and even the environment around us seem like enemies waiting for an opportunity to attack.

Modern people live day by day in this blocked and suffocating reality. We are trapped, without any hope.

A few years ago there was a shocking story in Japan. One day, a group of senior executives from big companies suddenly disappeared. Later, they were found working as day laborers at a countryside hotel, tidying the shoes of guests using the spa.

When asked why they chose to do this even though they had graduated from top universities and had good social positions, they said they disappeared to be free; they found it hard even to breathe due to the stress from their work and their families.

But the question is: even though they fled from reality to the countryside, were they able to gain freedom in their lives?

If you cannot get over problems in reality, in the place where you are living now, it will be hard to attain freedom no matter where your body is. If your consciousness makes a decision, your body and mind move accordingly, so you must first solve the situation in your consciousness, no matter whether your body is in an office or on a mountain. If your consciousness doesn't achieve freedom, you will not be able to find it either, even if your body is in the most remote and tranquil location.

Therefore, you have to learn how to get that real freedom that enables you to overcome all the suffering this reality brings. You cannot solve the problem by running away from reality. Wherever you are and whatever you do, you have to discover how to live a free life, without restraints.

How do you find the way to great freedom? Many people have tried.

Tao is the ancient Chinese concept of taking a journey to live in the right way and achieve spiritual perfection. In order to realize the truth that can solve the problems of our lives so we can live in great freedom, it is very important to find a master to show the right way. Since the beginning of history, many people have sought this great freedom, but found it too hard. This was because they never had the opportunity to meet a master who could guide them on the path to enlightenment.

Sakyamuni Buddha showed people how to reach enlightenment using a simple method that had nevertheless been very hard for him to discover, as it was then unknown. When taking the unknown path we have no choice but to wander. But the one who arrived first at the destination is able to lead others in order that they bypass the same trials and errors.

But because the tradition of truth-seeking has been disconnected and enlightened masters no longer appear via the religion and spirituality of modern times, it can seem like a comedy in which the blind are leading the blind. People seek only the methods allowed to them by religious doctrines, and practice technique using nothing but the shells of ancient saints. If they are deceived by the means (*upaya*), they cannot be enlightened but only cultivate the technique, even though they practice all their life. This is why it is vitally important to meet an enlightened master. It is so difficult to become enlightened only through vaguely practicing unconditional faith, praying, mantra, meditation, *hua-tou*, zen, yoga, and *danjeon*-breathing (transferring the breath into *qi* energy), without the correct guidance.

In order to meet a true master, you first make your mind empty. The problem is that modern people have too strong an ego. For a long time they have made their own religious dogma, creating fixed ideas that have stuck in their minds. This became like another ego. For innocent people, like children, the truth is easy to understand. But due to the complex human brain, they are distracted from being enlightened as they grow. What is the use of having many confusing terms when trying to attain the original true nature? Only by experiencing the truth in your heart—"There is no 'self' as an independent individual in every being of the phenomenal world"—and staying on the middle path, cutting off all dualistic discriminations, can you gain the realization of "no-self," a state of never being under the delusion, "I am."

After coming back from practicing in Myanmar, I wrote a book, *Ultimate Enlightenment*. I felt deeply that the first necessary thing on the path to enlightenment is to set up the theory of truth by teaching meditation to the disciples for one year. While giving lectures on the subject for four to five hours a week, I came to look at the truth almost as if through a telescope or microscope.

This book consists of the notes from these lectures, plus core content selected from my already published work.

We can see the truth fully when we acquire the ability to see both the woods as a whole and the trees as part of that whole. The obsession over self has to be cut off through practice, and the mind also has to disappear. Then we can see all phenomena that appear and disappear, within and without, as they are, realizing the no-self, originally no-I, in an unshakable state free from restraints. But in reality, most modern seekers of truth are in a pitiable state.

There are many worldly, enjoyable things to occupy the ego and the complexity of modern civilization wants us to be involved in it. So many people have no time to turn their eyes to the truth while they are struggling to keep up. Even if they jump into the world of seeking truth after having realized the vanity of material things, power and reputation, the situation is still not easy. To seek the truth is harder than finding a needle in a giant haystack. Religions with a long tradition, as well as the newer religions, have the same function of making a stronger ego.

How can we find bright eyes and open ears in a time of confusion, when we have already become too distracted?

There are only connections.

Now, in the fullness of time, the truth has met that precious relationship and has come to be known to the world. It is much appreciated.

I am deeply thankful to Gagil for his translating the manuscript for this book and also extend my gratitude to Eugene Campbell for his editing of the translation and to Boraun for her financial support.

Muwi Haegong
at Jeju Island, South Korea

Contents

Preface 1

Ultimate Enlightenment 9
    What Is the Truth? 11
    The Absolute and the Relative are One 43
    Cycle of Rebirth and Cosmology 58
    The Secret of Time and Space 77
    Dependent Origination with No-self and Individual Rebirth ... 88
    Distorted Words of Truth 108

The Path of the Seeker 121
    What is Enlightenment? 123
    The Moment of Enlightenment 136
    Verification of Enlightenment 183

101 Wisdoms 197

The Song of Enlightenment 229

Glossary 243

Ultimate Enlightenment

What Is the Truth?

If we don't understand the real concept of the truth, even though we may have been practicing, meditating and cultivating spiritually for a long time our effort may well be in vain. It is a pity that many seekers, even including Buddhist monks, have not been enlightened because they have been cultivating their minds and bodies, often through great hardships, in the wrong direction. This is why I must begin by establishing the right concept of truth.

But before we talk about what the truth is, let's think about the fundamental question, "Why do we have to be enlightened?" This question is very important, but impossible to answer in one word. Why should we realize the truth? Why do seekers throw away all worldly temptations and go on a path to enlightenment that will be very hard and which maybe nobody will recognize? There must be a purpose and a reason.

The first reason is to remove the suffering of life. For that, Sakyamuni, the Buddha, was looked to as a model. The reason Buddha renounced the world was to resolve the issue of suffering from being born, getting old or ill, and dying, which is the fundamental problem to face during life as a human. Buddhism says, "Life is the sea of suffering," because in life, a person is born and then must die. Suffering comes from clinging to our lives, which appear and thus must disappear. If things were meant to be born and live forever it would be no problem. However, all beings that are born and exist in the phenomenal world, such as animals, plants and even a stone, have to disappear.

Why do people suffer continuously? Because they cling to this impermanent and vain life. They cling to a life that appears and then disappears. Because it is 'my' life, I cling to it. The root of so much suffering in this world starts from 'I'. Because we cling to the delusion that this body-mind is 'I', the sufferings follow us. Therefore we come to lose happiness and freedom along with life. You might dispute this by saying, "No, I was happy, free and still alive, so I have life," but happiness, freedom and life from the point of view of truth mean a permanent state. The happiness, freedom and life you have felt in living are not permanent but only for a short moment. The impermanence of them makes humans sad and creates suffering. The one and only reason we seek the truth is to attain permanent happiness, freedom and life.

To do so we have to understand the fact that this body-mind is not the original 'I'. We are deluded by thinking our body and mind is us, but this is not the case. When we try and cling to the world around us, whether in the form of people, materials, honor or power, those things will not follow our volition.

The difference between the enlightened and the unenlightened is this—the enlightened one does not harbor the delusion of 'I'. Therefore they do not want to chase momentary happiness, freedom and life through this body-mind. The true 'Self' shares its original true nature with the Absolute rather than this body-mind; it never clings to something that stays for a moment then disappears like dust. That which we can really call 'I' is the only true nature.

What is a truth-seeker?

In the view of truth, there is no difference between Buddha and other sentient beings, including seven billion people on Earth. However, taking a perspective of phenomena in the relative world, we can classify four main groups of truth-seekers. In a pyramid shape based on that classification, we can find the laymen comprising the largest part on the bottom level. The laymen are seeking material possessions. The second level contains religious people, including non-religious groups such as those who practice *dan*-breathing, *ki*-practice, Taoist magic, etc., as well as traditional religions.

Laymen and religious people see differently in terms of material things and spirituality, but they are the same in their pursuit of happiness for themselves, centered around ego. A layman is in pursuit of the material and the physical, while a religious person is in pursuit of the spiritual and mental ego. Pursuit of spirituality may seem like a more noble cause than that of material things, but both are entirely based on ego. Ego means 'individual self,' for themselves alone, no matter if they are laymen or religious people. They live for their own happiness or that of their family and their own groups. Therefore most all religions these days are addicted to praying to God for mercy.

The pursuit of these religions and spirituality is the same as the pursuit of material things. When you realize the reality of this, then you are able to get past this level of the pyramid, to the truth-seeker level.

What is a truth-seeker?

A truth-seeker is a person in pursuit of pure truth. Though many people say, "I am a truth-seeker," in fact true seekers are very rare. Most are only in pursuit of material, spiritual and mental happiness. They call themselves seekers because they believe in religion or fall into a world of spirituality, but a true seeker is not in pursuit of egoistic self-realization. Even fortune-tellers can call themselves ascetic or gurus. Those words should be used for only the enlightened one, because they mean a person becomes truth itself and therefore a master who can teach the truth.

When I say this, people ask, "Are monks and priests truth-seekers?" External position or job has nothing to do with it. Truth-seekers are people who seek a pure truth in an internal world, but they are not distinguishable from the outside. Pure truth means no self (the phenomenal no-self equals the Absolute, the true self). 'No-self,' the level without ego, is the one of pure truth. The people who want to arrive at that level are the seekers. Over 99% of seven billion human beings are in the range of laymen and religious people; on the other hand, the seekers in pursuit of pure truth are fewer than 1%. The people who are in pursuit of pure truth and who become the truth itself are Buddha, at the pyramid's summit.

People who reach ultimate enlightenment, like Sakyamuni Buddha, are too rare to mention as a percentage. But these days, there are many people who insist they are enlightened in Buddhism or in many other spiritual groups. There are even some groups in which anyone can be enlightened within a week. Why is such so-called enlightenment becoming common? Because there is no right definition of 'enlightenment.'

Let's look at its true meaning. True enlightenment means to awaken from the delusion caused by fundamental ignorance and to realize the true nature of things. As soon as we realize 'no-self,' the true nature, we become a Buddha. That is ultimate enlightenment.

But according to Buddhism, enlightenment signifies "sudden enlightenment and then gradual practice." This means that enlightenment comes first, then becoming a Buddha can come about after all karma is removed gradually. But such enlightenment cannot be true enlightenment. Why do the seekers practice? Are they not practicing for enlightenment? But even famous monks of Buddhism insisted on that gradual practice, due to their delusions. They said, "I have already become enlightened but have not yet become a Buddha." And so they have to keep practicing. They distinguish being enlightened from being a Buddha. In fact, if you realize the true nature, become enlightened, then you will have become a Buddha.

You already realized who you are when you became enlightened, but now you need to practice more? After you have realized no-self, the ultimate enlightenment, you cannot be deluded again. So being enlightened equals being a Buddha. Then why do people say that they didn't become a Buddha even if they are enlightened? Because they didn't gain ultimate enlightenment, but merely some knowledge. They only understand true nature intellectually.

But enlightenment can be understood not in the head, but only in the heart. 'Heart' in this sense means the center of an existence, an existence not of an individual being but of the true nature. An unenlightened person sees themselves as an individual; they cannot understand what an enlightened one says because they try to fit it under their own frame, the ego.

When an enlightened person says 'I', this means the true self, the true nature, but unenlightened people understand it as an individual 'I'. Therefore they give irrelevant answers to questions and their words fall on deaf ears. They cannot understand each other—it is like the old saying, "When I point at the moon, why do you look at the finger, not the moon?" Even when using the same word, they can only understand it within the confines in which they are locked.

And the key reason that people become deluded is the wrong expression of "being a Buddha." Because they see it as "attaining Buddhahood," they cannot help being bound to those words. Enlightenment never means that an individual self completes themselves as a Buddha. This question will continue to be explained.

The limit of individual consciousness

If you understand how many levels there are in an ego, the limits of consciousness, you will come to discover a lot of interesting facts naturally. We call it an individual consciousness, or an ego. We recognize ourselves as an individual entity 'I' after being born. This consciousness of 'I am' evolves and grows, and its limit extends to become 'family.' Therefore the first level of consciousness can be called 'individualism' and the next 'familism.'

The confines of an ego can also get bigger. If the family extends more, it could evolve into the concept of being a region, and we call this 'regionalism.' If it gets bigger still then it might extend to the nation—'nationalism.'

Confines on the spiritual side, however, are known as 'religionism' or ideology. If extended further, 'humanism,' beyond religion and ideology, will appear, followed by 'life priority theory,' which features a respect for all life forms. At last the ego will reach 'cosmopolitanism,' the furthest limit, recognizing the universe as one.

This highest state, the furthest that ego can be extended can be expressed as, "I am the universe." Most seekers who misunderstand enlightenment fall into this category. Their consciousness becomes like a piece of puffed rice and they think of 'I,' just a small dot, as a universe, the biggest thing in the phenomenal

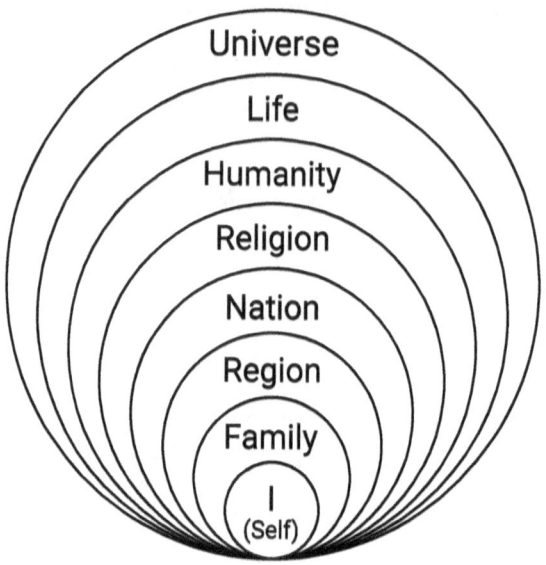

world. This is called the maximization of an ego. To egoists, such people are looked upon as having a great mind, because they appear different in scale. A person thinking of themselves as merely their body is at the scale of a glass of water and a person of universal consciousness is at the scale of the Pacific Ocean in comparison. It can be said that the scale of consciousness depends on the place in which one stays.

But surely this universal consciousness, as the biggest, must be enlightenment? No, this is just the maximization of an ego. Then what is enlightenment? It is no-self. That means a self doesn't exist.

No-self exists originally, not by the removal of self. But how is it possible to say "there is no-self originally"? What kind of state is self? It means there is originally no 'I,' no individual entity as a relative existence. Even though 'I' can continue expanding to be a cosmic consciousness, there will still exist 'I' at its center. Therefore ego continues to delude itself. What could be a greater delusion than saying that a self becomes a universe? It is the same great delusion as believing one's self to be enlightened.

At first, one thinks of oneself as small and only later deludes oneself as having become great. This is not true enlightenment, and in fact there were many cases like this in India, China and Korea through history until the present day. For example, Ramtias, an Indian mystic, thought himself to be the cosmos after realizing cosmic consciousness. Therefore he felt his body was a burden and decided to walk into the Ganges to drown. He recited a poem as he did so:

> *I became a cosmos.*
> *Now I feel this body as a burden, unnecessary.*
> *So I am going to return it.*
> *Now no confine is necessary for me.*
> *I became an infinite Brahman.*

This story has been told repeatedly—it was a famous event in India—but people cannot judge how they should understand it, or whether he was really enlightened or not. However, an enlightened consciousness would immediately know, because it recognizes true enlightenment: He deluded himself. He died through the delusion of an inflated individual consciousness.

Youngyun, a zen master, realized the universal consciousness and came to understand that all are one. He became to think of the universe as 'I.' He thought all things in it, even humans, ants, stones, water and fire was 'I.'

His consciousness grouped all things together. Once, as he was traveling on a mountain path with some other monks, they came upon a spreading forest fire. The others ran away but Youngyun walked into the fire saying, "The fire and I are one." Such misguided notions of enlightenment can lead you like this.

Both the one who drowned in the Ganges River and the one who walked into a fire were brave. They transcended death, didn't they? Through realizing a universal consciousness, they were not afraid of death. So is anyone unafraid of death enlightened? No. If so, then all those who die for their nation or some other cause, like martyrs, would have to have become enlightened. If you misunderstand the truth, neither the individual nor the consciousness can be harmonious, because the consciousness is out of proportion.

Now, the enlightenment claimed by Buddhism is a universal consciousness that mistakenly thinks of realizing "emptiness" as enlightenment. Because practitioners experience the truth in their minds but not in their bodies, they try to cultivate both their bodies and minds. They try to make true nature into knowledge, to be one with the body-mind. This is called *jeomsoo* in Korean, which means to practice gradually, but it is a great delusion. These people never can be enlightened even through ten thousand years of practicing.

Today truth-seekers cannot be enlightened because they all try to do the impossible. They are trying to be one with the truth through cultivating their bodies and minds. It is impossible.

Let's take a moment to look at this question: Why can it not be deemed enlightenment when one experiences universal consciousness, the ultimate limit of the manifested universe?

What is pure truth?

Seekers say they are in pursuit of pure truth, but do they really understand what it is before they begin their journey? If they have the right concept of truth, then they have only to follow that path. But the problem is that they claim to be following the truth without knowing what truth actually is. We should not say, "This is the truth because the Bible says it, the Buddhist Dharma says it, or the founder of whatever religion I believe in said so." Because they don't set up the theoretical concept of what truth is correctly, they wander about and become a laughing stock. Even people who set themselves up as teachers can be wrong, then more people will end up learning their misguided truth in turn. The blind are leading the blind.

You became a seeker in order to become enlightened. You have to know accurately what you are pursuing if you are to resolve your problems around birth, old age, illness and death and be free without any suffering in your mind.

The truth is "the Absolute."

Lao-tzu talked about the Tao (the Way) in his Tao Te Ching, 1:1. "When you speak about the Tao as the Tao, then it is no more the constant Tao." Lao-tzu seemed to worry about whether or not to speak about the Tao. However, on the premise that the Tao comes before words, he felt able to talk. But to say what the truth is, it is necessary to use the concept of "the Absolute." You must feel in your heart the importance of the Absolute. If you discriminate against it intellectually but not in your heart, you never can even approach enlightenment.

What is the Absolute?

We usually think of the Absolute as the opposite of the relative, but it is not. The last part of the word for the Absolute in the Korean language means "the object" and this "object" refers to the relative. The Absolute means that the relative itself is disconnected. In order to be aware of something, we must exist relatively—that means both the seer and the seen must exist. If such relative cognition is not present, it is impossible to cognize relatively. Therefore the Absolute cannot be cognized by a relative individual consciousness. Let's now look at the deeper meaning of Absoluteness.

"The Absolute" cannot be cognized.

Cognition—knowledge and awareness—is possible when *I* as a cognizer and *you* as a cognized object exist. But as the Absolute is not divided, it cannot cognize itself. It is therefore the One. This One refers not to a numeric concept, but to the One as the whole. Because it is only one, it cannot be cognized.

One's own self is unable to see itself. An eye cannot see itself, nor can an ear hear itself. Being only one, singular, is a state impossible to cognize. This lack of awareness might seem like not existing. If something exists as a phenomenal being it needs to be cognized, otherwise it is not a phenomenal being. Thus, from the standpoint of the phenomenal world, something singular cannot exist. But, paradoxically, because it doesn't exist, it is reality. Reality is existence itself, which means true existence without change.

What doesn't exist is what actually exists: what does this mean? In order to understand, we have to look closely in detail at the word 'existence.' Existence means manifestation; that is what we call existence. Through manifestation, existence can be cognized. But what appears must disappear. Therefore, how can an existence that appears for a moment and then disappears be reality? Disappearance means no existence. How can the things that disappear be reality? Such things are just illusions that can exist only for a moment. Because the things, the beings, in this world appear and must disappear, from this viewpoint they are all the same, whether they live for one year or a thousand. Because they exist only in the moment of appearing and must disappear, they are not reality but illusion.

Therefore, in order not to disappear, they should not exist phenomenally. If they don't want to exist, they should not appear. Truth is likewise paradoxical. Reality means lasting permanence. To be permanent is reality.

The quality of true nature, the truth, is Absolute. Because it is Absolute, it is singular. Relative cognition of that One is impossible, so it would seem not to exist in the phenomenal world. And, in seeming not to exist, it is true existence. As impermanent things appear and disappear, they are all illusions. Therefore, simply speaking, true nature as truth, the Absolute, never dies because it is never born in a relative phenomenal world. So it is permanent.

However, people use the term 'permanence' in the wrong

way. They delude themselves that permanence means without end. Some in religion say if they believe in the right way, especially Christians believing in Jesus, after death they will go to Heaven and live forever, whereas if they do not believe they fall into Hell after death, enduring eternal suffering. In Buddhism, people's bodies die but their minds are reborn according to their deeds while living, whether they be good or evil.

Taking a close look at these words, they seem to mean that there is a beginning of a spirit but no ending. There are even some groups that insist there is eternal life with the body, a belief rooted in Taoism. They are convinced that if someone is born and cultivates his mind and body well, he can become a Taoist hermit, living permanently without bodily death. There is a religion misusing such theory, saying, "You don't need hard *ki*-practice to gain eternal life. If you believe in this religion, you will naturally have such life." Their interpretation of eternal life is that, even though there is a beginning, there is no end. How absurd!

After a beginning, an end is destined to follow. In the phenomenal world, all beings that are born, including humans, have to die. There is no exception. The Chinese king Chin-si, dictator in his world, sent servants to find an herb of eternal life, but he still ended up dead. He died because it was his destiny to die. What is born has no choice but to die. Even the universe must have an end because it began. That is the law of existence of the phenomenal universe of relativity. Beginnings and endings exist in pairs. That is the law of birth and death. To appear is to be destined to disappear. There does not exist 'no-ending' when there is beginning, and also there does not exist an ending if there is no beginning.

Permanence has no beginning and ending. There is no ending when there is no beginning. Therefore permanence does not exist in the world of phenomena. It is a big lie that if you believe in Jesus, you will live forever. How is it possible to live permanently? Some might say that, though the body being born is dead, it is the soul that will live forever. But the soul also is born; why, then, does it not die? If the body is born and dies, so will the soul. Saying otherwise comes from ignorance of the basic principles of the relative world. Many want to exist permanently, which would mean no beginning and no ending. That is a state in which there is no birth and, at the same time, no dying.

Sakyamuni Buddha after enlightenment said, "I am freed from birth-death." People seem to think this is so simple, but it does not mean, "I will not die," but rather, "I am not born and also not dying." Sakyamuni Buddha was born and died, clearly. Then what sort of enlightenment enabled him to say, "I am freed from birth-death"? This did not mean the body-mind escapes from birth-death after enlightenment, but that the true nature, true self, is never born and therefore never dead. True self as the absolute truth is a permanent being itself, without birth-death.

The Absolute is permanent. It is everlasting because it has no beginning or ending and no existence as a relative individual. 'No-existing' doesn't mean not existing in reality, but in the eyes of the world of relative phenomena it does mean not existing.

In view of the absolute truth, only this truly exists and so it is called reality. Reality means existing in reality.

Therefore an apt metaphor for the absolute truth could be a circle. A circle is one whole and has no start or end. There is no starting-ending point on a circle. But the circle itself exists. Because of circling without ending, it exists without start or end. In the case of emptiness, all things repeat the appearance-disappearance cycle endlessly within it, but appearing and disappearing is relevant to physical things, not to emptiness. Emptiness exists but is not cognized and has no start or end. So it is called 'true nature.'

Paul Tillich, a great theologian of Christianity, said that God is simply a religious symbol of the concerns of humankind, that because God as the ground of all beings is Being-itself, He doesn't exist.

The Absolute Truth as found by Paul Tillich does not manifest itself, but is the foundation of all beings, all manifestations. In Christianity this is called "the absolute knowledge of God," personalized, but the Absolute doesn't have to be so called because it is not an individual being. Gods in all religions and mythologies in history are only imaginary creatures made by human consciousness along the lines of the human image. The Absolute is the fundamental root of the life phenomenon in the manifested universe.

All life, the phenomenal universe, is from the Absolute, but as the Absolute is not able to manifest itself and be cognized. It has to appear as relativity, to manifest itself; all the key points are in the sentence above.

Now we need to understand the meaning of the Absolute and the relative. These days, religious people and truth-seekers do not understand the Absolute and the relative correctly. They get the meanings of the two words confused and in fact often use them as opposites. In these two words are the basis of Truth, as well as all existing beings in the phenomenal world of the universe projected by the Truth. The terms themselves, the Absolute and the relative, have significant meaning beyond verbal expression. Because the Absolute cannot be manifested by relative cognition and is not a manifestation as a phenomenon, we have to realize the Absolute by understanding the relative world.

What is the relative?

In order to realize true nature as Absoluteness, we need to understand the principle of the relative world, the phenomenal world into which the Absolute truth manifests itself. When we can understand it correctly, we come to realize true nature as the Absolute that we cannot cognize. Here arises a question: It would be good if the Absolute manifested itself as it is, but why does it appear complicated? As we said before, the Absolute cannot be cognized in the phenomenal world due to oneness, and also we cannot cognize it because it existed pre-consciousness, beyond the cognition system.

We have to try to understand the relative, so that when the relative is completely melted down in our hearts, then we will realize the Absolute. The Absolute, that cannot be cognized by dualistic discrimination, has to appear as the relative, cognizable, in order to manifest itself. That is the secret of the phenomenal world. When the Absolute manifests itself, it must appear as the relative. In Korean, this is called *saek* (form), the phenomenal world, and *gong* (emptiness), the world beyond the phenomenal. *Saek* is the objective universe that we can see and live in. Let's look at what characteristics the relative, the objective universe, has.

First, the relative has to be cognized. If it is not cognized it is not the relative. The concept of *gong* is in relative cognition due to being the reverse of *saek*. In order for there to be cognition there must be at least two things, because in the state of the Absolute there is no separation into observer and object and therefore cognition is impossible. There must be separation. However, a being divided into more than two is confusing. After one is divided into two, it has to be divided again—continuously. This perpetual division has eventually led to the phenomenal universe, and that is why the universe has become complicated.

Second, the relative has to exist.

As the Absolute is existence itself, it cannot exist as a manifested individual. But an object must be in a state of being due to being cognized. To be a being it must be born; it has to appear, to begin. And so it follows that if it appears, then it has to disappear. Beginning must follow ending—these can actually be thought of as a single word. If one of these two is absent, then the other also has to disappear. The concept of beginning exists due to ending, and ending due to beginning. Therefore all manifestations appear and disappear in pairs, because the relative beings need objects in order to exist. Theoretically they are all made of concepts of relativity. Relative beings must disappear after their appearance. Therefore the manifested beings are illusion, not reality, because of the ending that follows beginning. True existence cannot disappear. But all beings that we can see are illusional because they appear they must disappear.

These beings are not eternal but momentary, because they exist only in a short time between beginning and ending. Sakyamuni Buddha said, "All manifested beings of the universe become conditioned." That conditioning means they are momentary; that all manifestations are conditioned to be born and die. Because all beings in the entire manifested universe, whether any form of life such as human, dog, tree or even stone, must be born and die, they exist as momentarily conditioned. We have to resolve this mystery—why must these beings be illusions?

It is as the objective universe that the Absolute manifests itself. Why do all beings in that universe appear as illusions; why must they disappear? As we have already explored, true nature has to be divided into more than two in order to be cognized. Also, true nature appears as individual beings, relative existence by the law of "dependent origination"—that nothing exists independently of other things. There must be such a mediator, if A is to be born as B. A gives birth to B and then will at some point later be dead, then B also brings C into being and will disappear in turn. Continuing birth-death likewise indicates dependent origination, beings appearing in succession.

In the case of human beings, grandmother gives birth to mother and then mother gives birth to daughter, on and on through the cycle. Consider a tree, which produces a seed that grows to be another tree, that produces a seed again. The cycle continues. "Dependent origination with no-self," as discovered by Sakyamuni Buddha, means that no-self equals dependent origination and vice versa, not that no-self is separate from dependent origination. Dependent origination has two important rules.

First, one is born from another.

One cannot exist alone due to dependent origination. Any lives, including humans, cannot be born by themselves.

Second, one cannot exist by oneself.

If someone existed alone, they could not be cognized. In this relative world, they can be cognized only when existing relatively. So they cannot exist alone.

These two rules—that one cannot exist either for oneself or alone—are the basis of dependent origination. Something is born by another and exists with that other. Speaking simply, if there is no *you*, then *I* cannot exist. Then how can such a being be called "I" in subjectivity?

What is the subject? Whatever exists by itself and doesn't ever change can be a subject. But if it is born from another, exists with another, and eventually disappears, then it cannot be a subject. Phenomenal beings that keep changing and disappearing cannot be subjects. When we realize the law of dependent origination, we come automatically to realize "no-self."

"All sentient beings in the phenomenal universe that continue to live and die by the law of dependent origination have no self that has any independent existence of its own." That is "no-self." There is no self existing independently because all are manifested by the law of dependent origination.

Sakyamuni Buddha's first saying after enlightenment was, "That arises because of this arising and that disappears because of this disappearing. That exists because this exists, and that doesn't exist because of the non-existence of this."

The first sentence means that one cannot exist for oneself, and the second means that one cannot exist alone. This is "dependent origination with no-self"; the core idea of Sakyamuni Buddha. The central idea in India 2,500 years ago was Brahmanism. The basis of Brahmanism was a doctrine of reincarnation. But after his enlightenment Buddha realized there is no self. There is a cycling of birth and death, but it is governed by the law of dependent origination and so there is no subject in it. "A nature of self is empty" means that in all objective beings there is no subject to insist on "I." If there is a subject, it cannot die. So there is no I as a subject.

This understanding of dependent origination with no-self was a tremendous revelation, which demolished all the contemporary theories in India. But, over the course of many years, Buddhism was swept away by the strong waves of Hinduism. As a result, it became the so-called Hindu-Buddhism. Now in Buddhism, both the terms "no-self" and "cycle of rebirth" are used together. Buddhists say "no-self" while also saying "rebirth." Are the two able to coexist? Given *I-am-not,* who would be in a cycle of rebirth? Rebirth means there should be a subject within the cycle, and Buddhists believe that a spirit is a subject. In the laws of the phenomenal universe, however, all manifestations appear and disappear in pairs. And so, the pairing of spirit and body appear according to the relative law and disappear in death; that is truth. Their failure to understand such a basic principle means that many Buddhists are trapped in the darkness of ignorance, unable to gain enlightenment. Many Buddhist monks try to gain the enlightenment that appeared to Sakyamuni Buddha, but their whole lifetime's practice will be useless due to such lamentably distorted religious doctrine.

No-self means no karma and no karma means no cycle of rebirth. Then who am "I"? Who is the true me? From the phenomenal perspective is it no-self, and from the view of absolute truth is it true nature. The pure consciousness manifested from true nature is "I" as a subject, which is not divided into *me* or *you* from the whole. Then, what is "I" in the phenomenal world? It does not mean *I* as a subject but as a word in opposition to *you*, the relative concept in an objective world. Let's look more deeply at the above, because we are born as relative beings and live with a relative concept.

All sentient beings in a relative world are relative beings that have a relative concept, and those beings with relative concept have a relative cognition system. That is, the human consciousness is made as such.

Therefore all concepts used by humanity exist as relative pairs.

There is no exception in the above principle.

Let's look over several examples of relative concepts: I and you, the most basic relative concept, yin and yang, good and evil, right and wrong, beauty and ugliness, and so on.

Relative Concept			
I	you	love	hatred
man	woman	pleasure	sorrow
Yang (+)	Yin (−)	sentient	insentient
is	is-not	interest	disinterest
material	non-material	knowledge	ignorance
good	evil	coexistence	incompatibility
sacred	worldly	cause	effect
birth	death	meet	leave
beginning	ending	bright	dark
beautiful	ugly	past	future
host	guest	time	space
body	function	eastern	western
black	white	primitive	civilized
cold	warm	parents	child
day	night	husband	wife
inside	outside	genius	fool
old	young	senior	junior
strong	weak	sky	earth
spirit	body	big	small
Buddha	layman	much	little
Nirvana	defilement	long	short
Heaven	Hell	high	low
angel	devil	deep	shallow
happy	unhappy	clean	dirty
truth	false	light	heavy
peace	war	slow	fast

I and You

I, in the relative world, means the counterpart opposite of *you*. If there is no *I*, then *you* also doesn't exist. These two words exist in pairs. When one disappears, then the other also disappears—that is a relative concept. Because the standard itself is a relative concept, such words are used only as relativity. If this *I* were the subject, the Absolute, what would happen? A subject cannot change from being a subject. In any case, in the final reckoning there must always be the absolute *I*. Only when I say, "I" does this use of *I* become who I am, become me. If I say, "I lent money to you," then how will you respond? You might say, "When did I borrow money from you?" Immediately who the *I* is, or was, changes into *you*. If I were the subject as the Absolute, then how could it change so? Whenever the speakers switch back and forth, this change occurs from *I* into *you*.

Here we are able to understand the delusion. Any identity that has been entirely believed as "me" can exist only as a relative and subjective concept, not as an absolute one. A being *I* does not exist in reality. If this were *I* by the Absolute standard, then others would have to say to me, "I" when they address me. You always must be you. However, depending on the other being in the interaction, words will probably be reversed. *I* becomes *you* and vice versa; in turn continuous change occurs. There is, therefore, no fixed *I* and *you* in the relative world. This is the identity that we have until now assumed—this body-mind as the constant *I*. Not at all. "I" is only a concept.

Then how is true nature the Absolute? As it is only one, there is no separation into *I* and *you*. But in the relative world, there must be this concept of *I* and *you* in order for existence to be cognized, and this concept persists when true nature manifests itself into innumerable beings. It happens only when it exists in the relative, or phenomenal, world. If it disappears from the phenomenal world, such dualistic discrimination will cease.

Yin and Yang (Negative and Positive)

In the relative world, a being can manifest only as a relative existence. Due to manifestation as relative beings, concept of these beings also has to appear relatively. All sentient beings in the phenomenal universe manifest as forms of yin and yang. For example, people exist as men and women, while there is male and female in animals, stamens and pistils in plants, and even in a single cell of asexual reproduction there exists yin-yang together. But it is not as simple as it appears. Does a man who looks externally like yang consist only of yang? Does a woman consist only of yin? If so they could not exist.

A being itself can exist when it already embodies relativity through the harmony of yin and yang. For example, women and men are individually yin and yang, yet each also consists of a combination of yin and yang together. This is the profound world of relativity. Eastern philosophy explains the human body in terms of yin-yang and the five elements theory. The human body can be sustained by the harmonious energy of yin and yang within, and by this yin-yang, male-female harmony all life preserves its own species. Look at the universe at large: it moves according to the harmony between yin and yang.

From the tiniest dust to the huge universe, all beings exist through the harmony of yin and yang. The important thing is, because all beings exist by the law of yin-yang, they consist of yin as a seeable or visible body and yang as an unviewable soul. Whether that soul is said to be mind or spirit, it has the same meaning.

But the meaning of the word "spirit" is different between East and West. The spirit in Eastern philosophy means both *jeong* as a body and *shin* as a soul complex. The *jeong* as material and the *shin* as soul produce *ki* through the harmony between them. *Jeong-ki-shin* is understood to be spirit from the Western standpoint, but in Eastern thought it is already understood as a body-mind complex or unit. The *jeong* is yin energy belonging to the body and the *shin* is yang energy and invisible. When these two meet and balance, there emerges an energy wave; that is the *ki*. If yin disappears, yang also disappears, because yang is the opposite of yin. It is the relative concept that one will disappear and simultaneously the other disappear.

Now, all people including the religious have mistakenly believed that body and mind are separated, and therefore yin and yang also split off individually. But they are separated only in concept; it is impossible for them to exist individually. With the proper understanding of the yin-yang principle, all the questions of matters like Heaven and Hell in Christianity and the eternal cycle of rebirth in Buddhism will be resolved.

Yin and yang are born together and will die together. Birth and death in pairs. Think about electricity—a light will come on only when anode (+) and cathode (-) are in contact. As soon as anode and cathode are separated, the light will disappear. Only by the contact of cathode and anode does the life phenomenon of electricity manifest. If they are separated, then the phenomenon will disappear and anode-cathode as a paired concept cannot exist anymore. In other words, body and mind are born in pairs, born simultaneously according to the yin-yang principle. They exist harmoniously and as soon as they die, the existence of body-mind disappears simultaneously. It is born in pairs, lives in pairs and dies in pairs. This is an inevitable law and truth of the existing world. These pairs are impossible to separate; one disappears and so does the other, at the same time.

Throughout history, there have been many unexpectedly comical incidents in religious gatherings under the flag of ignorance. For example, the story that medieval Catholic priests gathered to discuss seriously the topic, "How many angels can attend on the light of one candle?" Moreover, from the medieval to the present, there comes a more serious topic of discussion; when exactly does the soul come into the womb during pregnancy? Debaters of these questions are wasting their time because they cognize the body and soul not as a pair but as individual subjects.

When the body appears, the mind also appears. When the body disappears, the soul also disappears. But Christianity says that, even though the body dies, the soul will not die but go to Heaven or Hell after God's judgment. In Buddhism, the body is believed to be absorbed back into the soil after death while the soul will be reborn as a rich and noble person if they have demonstrated good deeds during life or, conversely, as an animal in the case of committing bad deeds.

Why do people believe in these ideas? Religion has brainwashed people, who do not know the relative law of the phenomenal universe, let alone the Absolute; the law of birth and death in pairs. Why don't people know such a simple principle?

Why do they believe in the theory of eternal cycle of rebirth? It is because of ego. The death of the body is too much for them; the disappearance of the soul scares them out of their senses, and so they believe in the eternal life theory. But what can we do? Our body-mind cannot help being born and dying together due to the law of birth and death in pairs.

Some 2,500 years ago, Sakyamuni Buddha realized the truth through practicing Vipassana: all phenomena in the universe exist by dependent origination with no-self. He said, "because of birth and death in pairs, there is no-self originally within individuals, and the self-nature in all phenomena of life is empty."

Beauty and Ugliness

What is the standard of beauty and ugliness? We say that someone is beautiful or ugly, but what is the basis for that judgment? The standard will differ depending on individual perceptions. Even when you think someone looks ugly, there will be someone else who is crazy about that person. Some people favor skinny people, some heavier people, some prefer tall people while others like shorter people. If there is a standard of beauty and ugliness, surely there might be differences within it? However, even a standard like this has to be relative. Everything is this way.

If there is also a standard of right and wrong, why do people fight each other? There is no absolute standard, so people are fighting every day, saying "I am right and you are wrong." Each insists they are better than the other.

Good and Evil

Today many people are confused by the concept of good and evil. Every religion has emphasized the good, saying, "Be good to people," "Do good," or "If you live an evil life, you will be punished." Let's ponder this. Is there any standard, any way to distinguish good from evil? When there is a standard, can we live a good or an evil life? I thought deeply about this before being enlightened, because I wanted to live a righteous life.

But nevertheless, there was no standard. What is the limit of good? What is the limit of evil? It was impossible to find the standard. Why is this so? Because the concept itself is relative. If you can establish a fixed line between good and evil, then it might be an absolute standard, because it could not be changed under any situation. But there cannot be such a standard. As all concepts in this world are relative and can exist only as relative concepts, a standard also is not absolute but relative.

The standard will be different depending on situations, people, and countries. Why are laws necessary? If there is an absolute standard, why is it necessary to make a law in every country? Due to there being no such fixed standard, there are different laws depending on customs, cultures, values, and situations. Korea makes its own laws according to its situations, as does the USA, as does Nigeria, as does Australia… the list goes on. In some Arab countries, one man is allowed to be married to four women. That is a law in those countries. But if an Arabian man tries to do this in Korea, then it is a different matter. This is because of different standards. Something that is welcomed and accepted in one place can be a big problem somewhere else, and vice versa. This is due to there being no absolute standard.

However people mistakenly think this relative standard of good-evil as absolute. When we say, "That person is good," what are we basing this on? It is just personal standards.

In fact, good and evil are just another example of a concept existing in a pair. Today all religions naively say, "Let us make a good world," or "Let us construct Utopia," or "Let us build a Buddha field." In any such world there will really be good. But if an evil disappears, what will happen to the good? It will no longer be sustained. Good is the opposite of evil, so if an evil disappears, then a good also has to do so. But if those two words disappear at the same time, can this relative universe exist? It will be impossible. So long as this manifested universe exists, a good and an evil have to exist in pairs. Simply speaking, as long as you exist, the body and the soul will, together. As the soul cannot exist alone after the body is gone, so good and evil have to exist together as long as the manifested world exists. That is truth.

Therefore, so many concepts that exist in pairs, like good-evil, you-I, yin-yang, beauty-ugliness, right-wrong, etc. can never disappear. Why is that so? Because if one disappears, the other also disappears at the same time—the manifested universe itself will disappear. So as long as this universe exists, such relative concepts as yin-yang, you-I, good-evil have to exist together. As all these concepts appear according to the principle of the relative manifested universe, a good and an evil have to exist together. That is truth.

Therefore, if good is truth, so is evil. But people want to drive away evil. The evil nonetheless will not disappear because evil is also truth. Both good and evil are truth within the relative manifested universe. You might think it would be a big problem if evil does not disappear, but you don't need to worry. Though those two concepts exist together in this manifested universe, they are just illusions from the perspective of true nature because they exist not as reality, but as concepts. They are only concepts created by the necessity to sustain the relative universe.

But people are suffering due to the illusions from these relative concepts. Then how shall we view the world? We have to view the world as it is, the truth; it is the relative manifested universe in which the original true nature, the Absolute, appears or disappears.

The Absolute and the Relative

All relative concepts existing in the manifested universe, like good-evil, right-wrong, beauty-ugliness, etc., are true nature itself, the truth. It is, therefore, foolishness and ignorance that cause dualistic discrimination.

People do not see the relative universe manifested as one of the whole, part of true nature, and so fall into using the relative concepts to exercise dualistic discrimination with the individual consciousness in the body.

By "dependent origination with no-self," no being exists by itself and alone in this relative manifested universe. So there is no subject to be named as "I." All beings must be born and die as they are beings of illusion and dependent origination with no-self. Why are they illusions? Because they have to change and disappear. These illusions exist, stay, and disappear under the principle of dependent origination.

That is caused by this and this is caused by that; one makes another exist and then disappears. A relative being cannot exist alone, but can exist only with an object. Therefore we cannot say such a thing as "I." What we can say is "I" is true nature, the Absolute, one that does not ever change, has no beginning and no ending, is not this and not that, but also is this and that. This is the only true "I." A being manifested from true nature is an appearance of illusion and only seems to be divided by relative cognition when manifested. But it is not really separated, it only seems to be separated when an individual consciousness is deluded.

Something that is only oneness is unable to be cognized and unable to exist phenomenally. But it appears as consciousness when manifested phenomenally. However, an unrealized person thinks of only his body as *I* and others as *you*, so his individual consciousness is divided. This divided consciousness comes from the individual consciousness that cognizes the individual as *I*. But in effect such consciousness comes from only relative concepts—there is no such thing in true nature, reality. Truth is the One, existing intrinsically in pairs.

The Absolute and the Relative are One

I have already explained the basics about the Absolute and the relative.

Firstly, it is necessary to explain the Absolute and the relative separately in order to make the two concepts understood, even though they are originally one. Therefore, as long as people cannot see the totality they are trapped within the limit of concepts. Though many truth-seekers, including Buddhists, say that the Absolute and the relative are one, actually they cognize that the two are separate. They misunderstand that the Absolute means an unmanifested empty state.

Let's explore what the Absolute and the relative are in reality and how they can become one.

The Absolute and the relative are not two but one. Eastern philosophy explains them as concepts of *mugeuk* (boundlessness) and *taegeuk* (yin-yang).

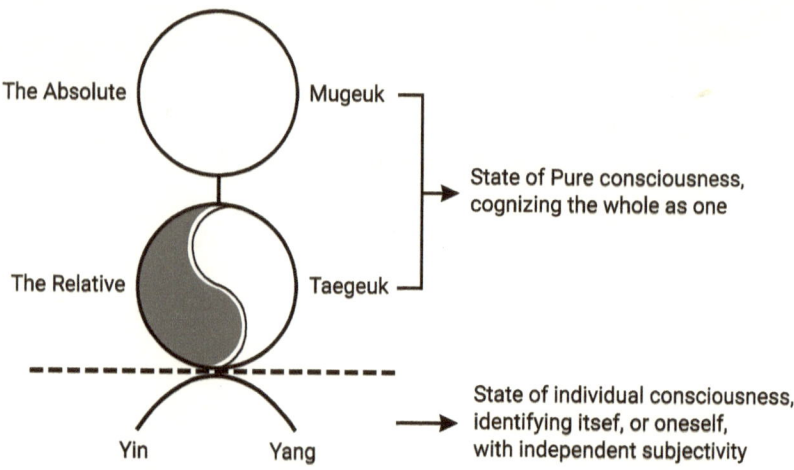

There is *mugeuk*, the source, from which there comes *taegeuk*, from which come yin and yang. These seem to appear in sequence but in fact are all within one. We describe it this way to explain it more easily. *Mugeuk* is the state of the Absolute in which there is no dualistic discrimination; *taegeuk* is the state of being yin and yang together, and the manifested world is a state of being separate as yin and yang through the manifestation of duality.

But you should not understand systematically that the relative comes from the Absolute and that yin-yang, of which there are innumerable forms in the manifested world, comes from the principle of the relative. This shows only the difference of cognition, not a sequence. To understand that the Absolute, the relative, and the manifested universe are one, let's change the picture.

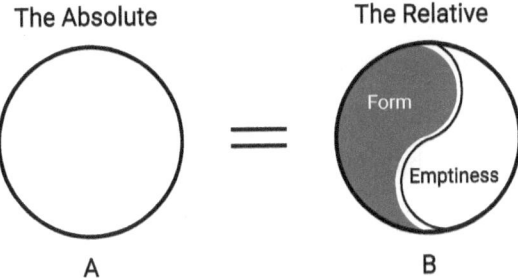

           A   B

Here is a universe. In the universe, the Absolute, there are two different natures: *saek* (manifested) and *gong* (unmanifested). The Absolute, which originally is one without dualistic discrimination, appears as relativeness, experiencing two different natures in order to cognize itself. We can call these natures *saek* and *gong*. *Saek* means the state of materiality and *gong* the state of emptiness as the opposite concept.

For example, suppose there is a room. When there is nothing in a room we can understand this state as *gong*. If material things appear like furniture or people, we see this as *saek*. Likewise, the true nature, the room, doesn't appear or disappear and is neither full nor empty.

What is it that appears and disappears? It is material things. In reality, only materials appear and disappear, not the room, which doesn't move whether or not there is material within it. It is therefore the same of the Absolute—there is both is-ness and nothingness, *saek* and *gong* all within. When there is a state of *saek*, it is within the Absolute, and when there is a state of *gong* it is still within the Absolute. The Absolute doesn't change but the relative concept within it changes. From *gong* to *saek*, from nothingness to is-ness, the relative concept changes.

But now many people mistakenly understand the Absolute as *gong*. They are deluded that it is the *gong* prior to the appearance of *saek*, due to viewing it as emptiness, nothingness. This understands only half of the Absolute. All exists within the Absolute whether it appears or disappears, whether there is a state of *gong* or *saek*. Nothing is outside the Absolute.

Buddhism sees the Absolute as emptiness. It is easy to think of a state of nothingness due to the expressive nuance of this word, but, as already explained, material things will be manifested with the help of emptiness. So, due to the appearance of material things, does the emptiness disappear? Or when material things disappear, does the emptiness appear?

It is not the emptiness, but the materials within that emptiness that appear and disappear. If you believe that emptiness disappears due to the appearance of material things, and that due to the disappearing of material things the emptiness appears, this is a delusion. It is ignorance caused by seeing the emptiness as *gong*, the opposite of *saek*, the state of non-existence of material things.

When we don't understand the truth correctly, we are often deluded. In fact it is very simple, but the Absolute will be divided into *saek* and *gong*, the relative concept to manifest itself, and *gong* will not be divided any further—*saek*, however, will be divided again into yin and yang due to the state of manifestation. So in a blink, it is possible to mistakenly understand the relation between the Absolute and the relative as that between *saek* and *gong*. The Absolute is not a state of *gong* but the state of wholeness, as One within which *gong* and *saek* exist together.

Let's take for example the difference in understanding the Absolute and the *gong*, the relative concept. Nisargadatta Maharaj expressed the true self as "a state of 100 years before you were born." But Ramesh S. Balsekar, his disciple, explained it as being like "0.01 seconds before the Big Bang." At first glance the two sayings seem alike, with Balsekar's simply on a bigger scale. There is however a subtle but significant difference between them. Balsekar cognized the true self as a state of no materiality, of emptiness, while Maharaj meant that, even though the universe exists, it is a state of non-cognition of an individual entity as 'I,' a state of no-self. Likewise the enlightened one cognizes correctly what the true self is, but the unenlightened one mistakenly believes the state of *gong* to be the true self, because he has not yet realized the no-self.

Let us compare it to a hand.

> Hand = palm + back of the hand

Let us take the palm as *saek* and the back as *gong*. When we see the palm, the back of the hand cannot be seen. Relative concepts have the same notional structure, so people can only cognize one side of the two poles. It is a tragedy: All delusions come from this. As soon as you cognize *saek*, the palm of your hand, you lose sight of the back, *gong*, which is hidden from your view. And when you cognize *gong*, the emptiness, you are not aware of *saek*, materiality, because the material world is hidden from your view. What happened? Between two poles, sentient beings always see only one.

This is why it is said that people always see only one side of the relativeness that the Absolute, original nature of truth manifests. Therefore their knowledge, concepts, and cognitive function render them into one-sided thought, inability to see the totality. That is the problem. If you cognize only the palm, you lose the back. But if you cognize a hand, you can understand both the palm and the back as part of it. The hand, of course, refers to the Absolute. The Absolute points to the whole. The whole of the hand is a hand, and when it is manifested in the world, it will be called individually the palm or the back of the hand due to the relative concept. Though it is originally a hand without mention of palm or back, due to its relativeness the one has to be divided into two in the manifested world.

Therefore, though a hand is cognized as either palm and back, if we understand a hand as one, with both palm and back, no matter which side we are looking at we can recognize that the other side is there too. But when we cognize only the palm of the hand we are stuck, and will never notice the back.

It seems everyone cognizes only the palm because only the manifested world can be seen, but the enlightened one realizes the hand itself. Such a person will know both the palm and the back of the hand. That means they cognize not only *saek* but also *gong:* They know that *saek-gong* exists relatively in pairs within the true nature, the Absolute; they know that *saek* and *gong* are both truth.

Returning to good and evil, therefore, if good is truth, evil is also truth. Both good and evil are truth existing in pairs in the true nature, the Absolute. When we see it as it is without dualistic discrimination, it is enlightenment. However, when there endlessly occurs dualistic discrimination like good and bad, we suffer continuously by being slaves to a concept that does not exist originally, because we cling to it.

Now, the important point we must know is that the Absolute is not some state before relative manifestation. It is the Absolute within which the relative concepts dissolve together.

Only when there is cognition will the Absolute be manifested as the relative. The *saek* in *saek* and *gong* does not continue in its same state, but will be divided again. It is, therefore, from here that relative concepts are born; you and I, good and evil, beauty and ugliness, right and wrong, etc. The biggest relativeness is the concept of *saek* and *gong* itself; *saek* means the phenomenal world, *gong* means a state of being empty, hidden, disappeared. Again, the relative concept, the yin-yang principle, will be manifested in this state of *saek*.

But *saek* and *gong* are only concepts—only the Absolute is a reality. So even though billions of individual entities exist separately in the Absolute, these are all manifested appearances from the Absolute, originally one. Therefore, if you cognize the truth you cannot be confused, because the Absolute and the relative are one. When you are disconnected from dualistic discrimination, from having a one-sided view and saying only this or only that, only then is there the truth, the Absolute as it is. Let us look over a few metaphors explaining this concept.

Sea and Waves

When wind blows over the calm sea it creates billions of waves and flecks of foam. If there were individual consciousness within a wave, it would think it was born when it was created. So when it lives and disappears, it would think in terms of being dead. But from the sea's perspective, although the waves continuously rise and fall, the One of the sea takes a changed shape only for a second but is still the sea. The wave doesn't exist separately from the sea. But if there were a consciousness in the wave, it would believe mistakenly that it is independent. It is the same when people delude themselves into considering themselves independent personalities.

The sea—true nature—is just the sea, before the waves arose, while the waves are arising, or after the waves fall. Therefore whether the waves appear and disappear, there is no change to the true nature, there is only a small change in shape. From the sea's perspective there is no birth nor death.

But when we focus on the waves, then the waves are born and die. So do men. If the consciousness clings to the individual, that consciousness comes to be the individual, and one thinks of only this entity as oneself, thus coming to the illusion that a person is born and dies. But the true "I" is never dead, as it was never born. There is only appearance and disappearance within true nature. This is called "never born and never died."

The true "I" is eternal truth, true nature itself, and within it billions of illusions appear and disappear. The waves rise and fall in the sea, but the sea itself remains either way. If we call the state of waves rising as *saek* and waves falling as *gong*, the sea itself is true nature, the Absolute.

It is very important where the confines of consciousness are located. The enlightened align with the sea's view. At the moment we are enlightened while living with individual consciousness, "Ah! I was originally the sea, not a wave." Thus we can know our true nature. Within the sea, even if billions of waves rise and fall, the whole is one.

Body and Cells

A body consists of trillions of cells. So if the cells each had consciousness, they would think of themselves as *I* and the other cells as *you*. And since each cell's average lifespan is three to four months, it might think, "I was born three months ago, so I shall live hard with my own will then die in a few days." In each cell's perspective, it is born, lives and dies. Have you ever thought that there are trillions of cells in your body, about how many changes are constantly happening to sustain the body? But we call "I" the whole that consists of billions of cells working in harmony, not a single cell.

Let us extend the consciousness more and consider the universe as a body. There are so many galaxies in the universe. The galaxy in which there is the solar system where humans live consists of 200 billion stars, so a solar system seems like a particle of dust. In that solar system, Earth is one of eight planets. Therefore by this measurement the "I" of Earth is vanishingly small. Comparing the universe with a human being, what is the difference between "I" as a being in the universe and one of the trillions of cells in a human body? And thinking of the time of the universe, can you say that a hundred years of a human lifespan is much longer than the three months of a cell lifespan in that human body? In the span of the universe's existence, a hundred years are just a moment.

People feel pity for the short-lived mayfly. But from the standpoint of the universe, humans are like mayflies. A human being as a cell in the universe keeps being changed as a part of a larger organic body, just as the cells in the body are continuously being substituted by new cells in three-four month intervals. This is the dependent origination principle in action.

However, you cognize not the whole but your body as "I," due to having an individual consciousness. Take the wave that has individual consciousness and thinks it doesn't exist when the sea calms—seven billion people on the earth are basically thinking the same way. When you cognize true nature, the state of One, i.e. the sea not a wave, the whole universe not an individual body within it, you understand that all beings are just circling within the One.

The enlightened person stays in this true nature, as pure consciousness not an individual, so they know that this manifested entity is not *I*, a changed phenomenon of true self, true nature. Though true nature is divided into billions of beings, the basic source is one. Even though these beings appear and disappear many times, the enlightened person knows this is only a kind of manifestation and never deludes themself into thinking that such an illusory phenomenon is their own self.

Then why is an individual consciousness, an ego, born?

If it stayed in the state of the sea, pure consciousness, from the beginning, there would be no delusion or confusion, so why does an individual consciousness appear? Why do we think of myself as "I" and the others as "you" with dualistic discrimination and thus live in suffering?

That is because the Absolute cannot help appearing relatively when it manifests itself. The moment when it is born as a relative being with relative concept in this manifested universe, it cannot avoid the separated concept of *me* and *you*. That is the inevitable fate of anyone and the truth of the phenomenal world. Therefore it is inevitable that people are deluded. All sentient beings appear as relative existences with relative concept when born, so everyone has to be a separated individual consciousness. However, when this individual consciousness is discovered by a being, pure consciousness, the "I" as the whole One, will appear.

That is to realize true nature, the original face. There is, therefore, no discrimination from Buddha among sentient beings for the enlightened. From the perspective of true nature, the Absolute, with consciousness of no-self, all sentient beings are Buddha. All is true nature itself. Only the roles assigned in the diversely manifested world are different.

Therefore the relative phenomenal world manifested from true nature is the truth as it is. The law of nature flows in the perspective of pure consciousness, without dualistic discrimination.

Finally let us summarize again how the Absolute and the relative function.

"I" as a Dreamer and "I" in a Dream

We dream during sleeping. In a dream there is an "I," an individual being, people around this being, and this world. During a dream, that individual self in a dream should be "I," undoubtedly. In the dream you will live with feelings of joy, anger, sorrow, and pleasure as usual. The moment you wake up, you will know that the "I" and the people around you in the dream were all illusions. And you surely know that you are the dreamer, not the "I" in the dream. Likewise, there are billions of characters in a dream, a phenomenal universe, that the consciousness creates. In that dream there must be one character who deludes themself as "I." At the moment of waking up from the dream, the character believed to be "I" will disappear without a trace and only the consciousness which dreamed will remain. Therefore I am the consciousness of the dreamer, not an individual entity in a dream. Only during the dream do I mistakenly recognize a deluded being as being me.

When you eat beef, the beef will be taken inside to become part of the body of a human being. The continuous circling of the food chain is echoed in the organic function of making the phenomenal universe exist and be sustained. There is just a moving from this body to that body. All sentient beings in the manifested universe are capable of taking other beings' lives. That is the truth. So we need to know that killing is wrong and comes from dualistic discrimination and the ego of humanity. Why do we say that animals have life, but plants don't? We have to throw away such a childish thought.

When we see a movie, the screen is a support. Without it the image will scatter in space. But with the support of the screen, the image will appear using the light shot through the film. There appear various scenes on the screen during the movie. Sometimes there is a fire or at other times people die in a war. But after playing the movie, all these scenes will disappear and only the screen, the image support mechanism, will remain. Any horrible scene manifested on the screen will not infect it.

Our original nature is like the screen. Although billions of beings and events are manifested in true nature, all things manifested will disappear soon enough. But true nature is always there, before the phenomenal universe was born or after it disappears. However, unenlightened people cling to a single scene and suffer as a result. All your lives, events and the karmic affinity of the past have already passed by. Only ignorant people are attached to the past in their minds, living in suffering. The future also doesn't exist because it is not yet manifest. For us there exists only here and now. When your consciousness remains always awake in the here and now, enlightenment will appear by itself. True nature will not be tainted in any situation. There is only a delusion that it is tainted. All things are a kind of play, a festival.

The Middle Way

It is the middle way that is disconnected from dualistic discrimination such as right-wrong, good-evil, etc. There is no reason to discriminate dualistically. Why? It is all the truth because all phenomena exist in pairs as relative concepts manifested from the Absolute. How can things that are not true come out? Although what is happening may seem not right from your perspective, it is the truth. To judge it not true is not the truth.

Cognition has to be in pure consciousness, staying within true nature. If you are able to be influenced, brainwashed and filled with blind faith by the individual consciousness in the relative manifested world, you cannot realize the truth.

Now let us sum up.

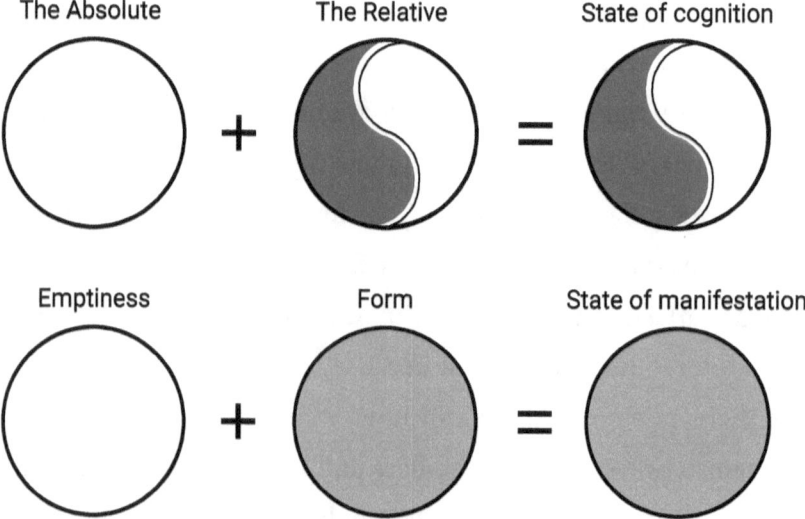

When you put together the Absolute and the relative picture, what does it look like? It will appear to be the relative objective world. But the basis of the world is the Absolute. The manifestation is relativeness, but the Absolute exists already in the foundation.

The Absolute cannot be cognized as an individual entity, but even though it is not cognized, not manifested, it exists and it is true existence. Manifested beings seem to exist due to being seen, but in fact they are illusions, due to being born and dying. All the explanations above should be understood deeply in your head. You have to realize that "I" as subject is not the body-mind complexity like the dust of the manifested world, but true nature itself, the Absolute.

In other words, cultivating the body and mind is not the right practice. Why do you cultivate the body-mind? The body-mind is not "I," but an illusion. True practice is to be aware of it as it is. All that pure consciousness manifested from true nature has to do is to become aware. If you see things as they are, here and now, you will know that all things arising in the body and mind—any thoughts, words, actions, emotions, senses—and all beings, events, and phenomena in the manifested universe have to be born and die. Because of birth and death, they are impermanent beings. When you understand impermanence, no-self will be realized within you, by itself.

Nowadays many spiritual truth-seekers try to cultivate their bodies and minds. It is because they think there is taint and ego in their bodies and minds. But the true *I*, the true nature, could not be tainted by anything due to its purity; it is clarity itself. That is the original face. Don't be deluded or confused. The true nature, the true *I*, is always clean, free, happy and peaceful. We have to realize true nature as the true self instead of suffering from dualistic discrimination and defilement within a small body.

Cycle of Rebirth and Cosmology

It is estimated that people began to have interest in the spiritual world five thousand years ago. A man suffering from a headache began to think about the afterlife, asking, "What will happen after death?" Such a question began to appear vaguely in his consciousness, but he could not answer it. Since then, cognition of the afterlife began to appear alongside spiritual evolution and the development of intelligence. During that time there emerged the concept of the soul as something different from the body.

The body comes from the soil and so goes back to it, but the existence of the soul was also believed even though it was not seen. It was thought that the body was a kind of vessel, or something like a house or a set of clothes, and the soul is within in. This soul was considered to come from someplace unknown, like the spiritual world or Heaven. People said that the body was like clothes that were either worn or taken off. After the soul has lived in the body, which is subject to decay, in the Christian tradition it goes to Heaven or Hell, depending on its deeds during life; that was an initial stage concept of the world after death.

At that time there was no concept of rebirth—it may have been beyond prehistoric people's capacity to envisage.

It can be called a linear view that there exists Heaven and Hell; a person is born, living until the time of death, and then goes to one of these places, all in a straight line. If one goes to Heaven or Hell according to how they behaved, then they will live there forever. So they have to live a good life after being born. Because there was no concept of the Absolute and the relative at that time, the idea of the soul came to take hold.

The theory of Heaven and Hell according to the good-and-evil concept came to form the basis of primitive religion and be accepted as the truth, but such cognition came to change with the development of human intelligence. Some wiser man said, "No. If one has to go to Heaven or Hell permanently after just one life it would be too cold-hearted. Giving him a chance through cycles of rebirth is fair." That was how a cyclic view began to emerge. People figured that mistakes happen all the time. Why, then, should someone go to Heaven or Hell forever just because of one decision? That should not be so, because the course of a life changes like the four seasons in nature.

From the cyclic view, the doctrine of cycles of rebirth came along, starting in India. The linear view of history went out of fashion and now the doctrine of rebirth is prevailing all over the world.

The main idea in the doctrine of rebirth is the immortality of the soul. There are two perspectives on this.

One is the linear view of history in which sentient beings go to Heaven or Hell forever. The other is the cyclic view of history in which they live different lives forever in the eternal cycle of rebirth. What is the entity of rebirth? People believe that it is only the body that disappears while the soul constantly revolves. If the cycle meant that a soul would return only as a human being, people would not be afraid to do bad deeds. Buddhists insist that living things should be reborn as one of the six samsaric destinies according to their deeds while they were alive. Buddhism's doctrine of rebirth includes these six samsaric destinies: being in hell, hungry ghost, animal, suffering being, human, and heavenly being.

Did Buddha say anything about these six samsaric destinies? No. Then who defined them? Buddhists believe in the 84,000 Dharma as being all Buddha's sayings. But that is not true. These Dharma were all made after Buddha's life. Christians believe in the Bible of 66 books as the words of God, but when did God speak the words directly? The truth is that humans wrote the Bible but insist upon it as the word of God in order to render it authoritative. When you read the scriptures of Buddhism, they are all written with, "I heard like this," at the beginning. This is because Anan, a disciple of Buddha, talked about Buddha's words, which he had memorized while standing always at Buddha's side at the original meeting for creating the scriptures of Buddhism. That was the start of the scriptures of Buddhism; Anan started to speak after saying, "I heard like this." Therefore Buddhists believe that if it does not begin with, "I heard like this," then it is not the words of Buddha. So, all the scriptures begin with, "I heard like this," even those written 1,000 years later. All this is because of authority.

When you see the Bible, you know that there is a name on every gospel, like the Gospel of Matthew or the Gospel of John. These gospels also were not written by these people, who were disciples of Jesus. Even though the New Testament was written 100 years after Jesus and his disciples, nevertheless these names were put on the Gospels. Through that the Bible could be seen as more authoritative and thus more credible. At that time people believed that if there was a name such as Matthew's on the Gospel, it would be true. But the modern study of paleography found the true chronicles of the Gospels. For example, though some insist that words or phrases were written 500 years ago, the real facts will be discovered by investigation: 500 years ago they did not use such words. At that time speech patterns were completely different. All this is revealed by paleographic research.

Therefore people cannot keep insisting on these as truths anymore. The saying "I heard like this" at the beginning of each Dharma can no longer be acknowledged as authoritative. If we examine the scripture of Buddhism or the Bible through paleography, the chronology will be revealed. Though Buddhists insist 84,000 Dharma Sutra were all words of Buddha, they have been revealed to have been made by Buddhist monks or scholars hundreds of years ago. The Mahayana Sutra, as believed in China, Korea, and Japan, may have been made up by each religious sect's particular explanation of Buddha's teachings, like all the other religions.

Anyway, although the doctrine of six samsaric destinies emerged well after Buddha, nowadays Buddhists must believe in that as his teaching.

Buddha never said the cycle of rebirth refers to individual beings. It is well known that no-self and dependent origination is the truth that Buddha realized. Remember what no-self and dependent origination mean? That no being in the universe can exist by itself, because it did not come into existence by its own free will. It also means things cannot exist on their own. In the relative world there must be a subject that perceives and an object that is perceived. Existence is possible only through relativity. Being A can exist only when being B exists. If B disappears, A will also disappear according to the law of relative manifestation. No being can exist by itself and on its own. Therefore, even if an individual does manifest, he does not have 'I' as subjectivity within. That means no-self. Why is this the case? Because an individual being is subject to dependent origination. If there is a concept of rebirth, we can consider it as the rebirth of dependent origination because, from the perspective of totality, one living being continues giving birth to another.

Nowadays, however, Buddhists believe rebirth in the sense that an individual is born, dies and will be reborn as a dog, a frog, a human, etc. Logically speaking, if all individual spirits including seven billion people on Earth rotate among each other, how could this happen? Subjectivity means that it can exist on its own and never change eternally, but when it is born without free will and cannot exist by itself, how can it be a subject? People are missing this simple notion.

The subject is only one and operates the whole. Though each of the trillions of cells in our body don't mean that much individually, the body cannot exist without the unity of those cells. From the perspective of the relationship between the whole and an individual, the term rebirth means that the whole revolves interdependently according to the principle of dependent origination. The eternal rebirth of an individual as a subject is impossible because there are countless entities of rebirth: animals, insects, etc., including billions of humans. All beings are illusions due to existence by dependent origination, because all beings in the relative world are destined to live and die, and birth and death exist in a pair.

All relative beings in the manifested universe exist in pairs as a relative concept. All living beings appear in the context of yin-yang. From a tiny dust mote to the entire universe, all beings exist in the harmony of yin-yang.

So this means that yin and yang, body and mind comprising an individual entity of relativity will be born simultaneously, live together, and die at the same time when there is no more yin-yang function.

Human beings cannot escape that principle. The moment that plus (+) and minus (-) are separated in an electric circuit, they will disappear simultaneously. It is impossible that only the minus will disappear and the plus will go somewhere alone to come back. However, people believe that the body dies, but the spirit will live in Heaven or Hell and be reborn with another body according to their karma. The body and spirit come together and go at the same time; then who will be reborn? Such belief can only stem from the egoistic mind because people do not know the truth and the law of existence in the manifested world.

There is therefore no rebirth, and so modern Buddhism does not hold up. And there cannot be Heaven and Hell due to no-self in individual entities, so Christianity will come to an end too. It is said by Taoism, Seon-do and *ki*-practice that we can live an eternal life through cultivating our bodies well. Is that possible? No. All religions and spiritual groups with these kinds of wrong teachings will come to an end. In the 21st century all such primitive thought will come to an end through a more rational evolution of human consciousness.

Then why are people praying to Buddha to be born in a better place after death, or donating money at church to get to Heaven? It can only be a kind of comedy.

We have to resolve the problem of living and death, and why the universe has it—because life does exist within the universe. We cannot know life without resolving the problem of the universe; neither can we understand death.

But the concept of the universe appeared about 2500 years ago and was only correctly understood less than a few hundred years ago. Before that there was no such concept, only one of sky and earth. At that time people thought that Earth had a quadrilateral shape surrounded by the sea, having an end because the universe, such as it was, was considered a flat structure. At first people believed in the geocentric theory; the sun rising from the east and falling into the west due to the quadrilateral shape of the earth. It was Copernicus and Galileo who changed this thinking with heliocentric (Copernican) theory.

The heliocentric theory means that Earth moves; that means

it is round. If the earth was a quadrilateral shape, how could it turn? The sun appears to be moving across the sky, but in fact Earth orbits around the sun. Earth turns from west to east, but to our eyes the sun looks like it is turning around the earth from east to west. That is a difference between manifestation and reality. People in those days believed that the sea has an end because it surrounds the land. The horizon when viewed seems to come to an end. So people did not like to go on voyages far away because they were afraid of falling off the edge of the sea. Magellan and Columbus broke that belief.

They went on a voyage at risk of their lives saying, "Let us go right to the end of the sea." But they kept on sailing and came back to the beginning. While Copernicus and Galileo posited the theory that Earth was round, Magellan and Columbus took personal action to prove that theory, and this happened only a few hundred years ago.

The concept of the universe began to take shape when science started to appear. In ancient times philosophy took the place of science. The noted Greek thinkers Socrates, Plato, and Aristotle were philosophers and scientists at the same time. At that time they could not prove their theories and so merely imagined them in their minds. For example, Plato suggested an imaginary world of ideology in his theory, Ideas. Later, when science developed, it separated from philosophy. This happened a mere 500 to 600 years ago.

Newton is known as the father of modern science. He discovered the famous universal law of gravity. When he was hit on the head by an apple dropping from a tree, he wondered why all things drop only from above to below. After studying the phenomenon he came up with the theory of gravity, the fact that the Earth pulls all things towards itself. People then realized that all things in the world have the power to pull towards each other, a universal gravitation; they applied the theory and proved it to be 100% correct. Therefore universal gravitation came to be recognized for quite a while as the eternal truth.

But at the beginning of the 20th century the theory of gravity was replaced by Albeit Einstein's theory of relativity. Why? Simply speaking, because the "theory of gravity" was only a relative principle, not absolute. There can never be such an absolute principle because all principles applicable to all materials in the universe function as relativity. It was an important realization and served as a tremendous leap of perception that became a landmark in the spiritual history of humanity.

The truth came to a collapse. The belief in that truth of philosophy, science and all humanity of the world up until the 19th century had been broken. It was done with just one different point of view or perspective. People observed things on Earth because they lived on the earth, believing that the principle of gravity was true. And yet, if you were watching from outer space, that truth could be applied only on Earth, like a frog in a well. Therefore the theory of relativity has become tremendously important. We can say that the concept of the universe only really started at that time. Science before the 19th century did not apply to the universe but only to Earth, supported by human-oriented ideas.

Einstein discovered the fact that even the speed of light

needs to be cognized by relativity. The speed of light is always the same in any place or situation, e.g. light from the headlight of a moving car or from a standstill. If I am riding on a spaceship able to fly at the same speed as light, does light seem to pass by or not? Light will not seem to move. But if I stand by the light passing by, I will perceive the light as tremendously fast.

Perception according to the sense of the body is all relative. The speed of light will not change but can be changed according to the situation of an observer. However, even the theory of relativity, which had replaced Newton's law of gravity and came to be believed as truth, has come to be replaced by quantum theory. Recently the unified field theory has been introduced, which should be absolute—and yet, it has not been completed by physicists.

While the theory of relativity is at the universal level but serves as the principle of the manifested world, the unified field theory explains that all physical entities, though seemingly different, are just one thing or substance, indistinguishable from each other. Therefore the theory of relativity is the principle only of the phenomenal world. There is not even any such principle of relativity if you explore more deeply all the way to the source. It is, however, another important discovery by Einstein that he replaced the theory as he had formulated it so far, in which all events happen by collisions between materials because of their manifested appearances. It is the materials that appear through the collision between events. That is, while the events are the source, the materials are manifested phenomena.

For example, if you turn on one of the early television sets that used a Braun tube, at first there appears a single dot and then pictures come out on the screen. That one dot comes from the combined events of collision among many light waves. But we cannot see the image in the collision between light waves, only the dot, and later we see the manifestations as pictures on screen. Simply speaking, the phenomena that we can see with our eyes are not the fundamental truth.

Science has now developed amazingly. It is, however, a limitation that science views the truth only from the perspective of the manifested world. It can only discover the truth of phenomena already manifested. But phenomena manifest in a state of relativity, that is only the form (*saek*). Can we discover the non-manifest? Through science it is impossible to do so. To discover the non-manifest we have to be able to observe it. It is, therefore, impossible for us to perceive any non-difference between the form (*saek*) and the empty (*gong*), the Absolute, due to our need to cling to manifested appearance. That is possible only through enlightenment.

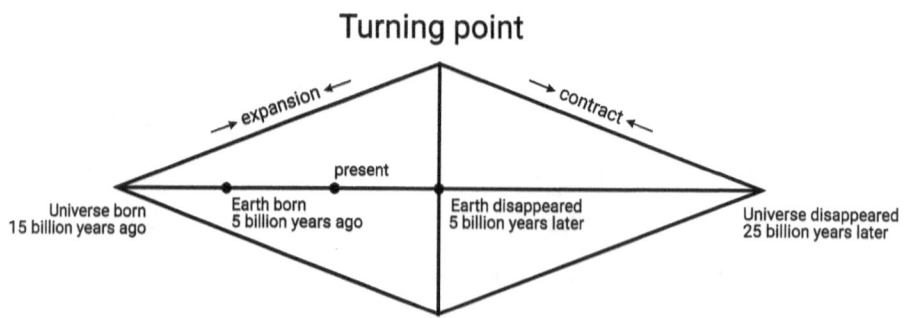

During the 1920s the astronomer Edwin Hubble discovered that the universe in which Earth exists is continuously expanding. How did he learn that? For example, the distance between two galaxies was measured to be greater upon later observation, proof of the expansion of the universe. Based on this expansion the history of the universe was revealed. It is said that the universe containing Earth was born from the Big Bang, starting from one dot, will arrive at the peak of expansion after some five billion years, and thereafter contract back to a point. This follows the law of relative birth and death. This is all in resonance with the truth. A cycle of the universe consists of four stages. It is like being born in spring, growing in summer, harvesting in fall, and going back to the origin in winter. The universe also is born from a dot, expands, reaches the turning point, thereafter contracts, and disappears. That is birth and death. It will be two stages at large, appear and disappear, and if split to four then spring, summer, fall, and winter.

In the case of humanity, we can also split into four stages: infanthood, youth, adulthood, and old age. Therefore the universe will begin to contract five billion years from now. It was discovered by Hubble's astronomy that the universe was fifteen billion years old and the earth was born five billion years ago, ten billion years after the universe was born. How could humanity exist without Earth? Of course we could not. However, could a concept of rebirth or Heaven and Hell be applied before the appearance of Earth?

It is due to anthropocentricism (human-centricism) that such concepts came about. Furthermore, Earth was born five billion years ago; did humanity begin to appear at the same time? It is said that *Homo sapiens sapiens*, modern humans, emerged just fifty to sixty thousand years ago. Before the appearance of living things, Earth was covered with primordial gas and dust. On this dusty planet a mysterious phenomenon occurred. It is called atomic motion in science and the conditions of earth, water, fire, and air in the philosophy of India. With the appearance of such conditions in the universe, Earth emerged as a planet on which living things could be born through the harmonious energy of the universe.

It was long widely believed that there was probably no life around the other stars except on Earth; that is, there was until recently no evidence of conditions for living things to evolve elsewhere, but Earth does have such conditions. With them in place, a minimum-substance life-form was born. Complex living things such as humans could not have emerged at the very beginning.

First appeared RNA and DNA in primitive pre-cell configurations. It was not an animal, not a plant, nor anything like extant existence as we know it. But there did appear living things from mineral matter. These single cells evolved into animals or plants in the conditions that existed in the primordial ooze formed of Earth's dust. The early primates, the origin of today's humans, are said to have evolved not only into humans but also other animals, including monkeys and gorillas, according to the conditions existing at the time.

Though the first single-cell units diverged into animals and plants, their first-life units were the same. And where did this first single cell begin to appear? It came out of the earth, the minerals in the mud. It means minerals, plants, and animals were originally all one. Likewise, through a long period of evolution emerged the higher animals and modern humans. While these humans may be thought of as higher animals, from the viewpoint of the whole truth they are not really very intelligent. This is because they do not know the totality of the life source and put everything into anthropocentric focus, the egoistic concept.

It is the same as if the theory of gravity were true in every respect, because Newton had a one-sided viewpoint. People have a human-centric view on cosmic history, and everything else. So, in the Bible's Genesis, God said, "Let us make mankind in our image, in our likeness, so that they may rule... over all the creatures," while creating human beings on the last day after creating the world. Who wrote that? Man himself.

Then people use that as the basis of their argument, saying, "Look, didn't God say this?" Even funnier are the people who believe in that word as the truth, who are also being exploited. From the perspective of the history of the universe, human history is very short; nevertheless people repeat such absurdities. Apocalypse proponents speak as if the end of humanity is equal to the end of the Earth, but Earth continued to exist in spite of the extinction of the dinosaurs. Similarly, Earth will remain unaffected even if all humanity disappears. Furthermore, even when Earth crashes into dust, the universe as a whole will remain.

It was a few hundred years ago that humanity began to

gain such scientific cognition. Before science came to the fore so substantially, people had believed blindly in every sort of religion. Why did Christianity sweep the world for 2000 years? Because there was no science. Though they said Jesus was born from a virgin, people believed it because there was no proof to the contrary. What could they say about the words of God? However, with the development of science, many people came to know that such an idea is ridiculous. Therefore Christianity is failing in the West, but notably it is still prospering in Korea. Buddhism is said to be superior to Christianity, and is now Buddhism is becoming more accepted in the West. It is, however, a pity that the truth of modern Buddhism is almost distorted. It says that individual spirits are reborn. How is this possible? It is the law of depending origination that shall rotate, in totality.

Here is the sea. When the wind acts upon it, waves rise and fall. One wave is a changed state of the inseparable sea caused by the condition of wind. Is it possible for a wave to have individuality, or not? If the sea is viewed as the universe and a wave viewed as a human, can the human be an individual entity?

From one universe appeared countless living things, changing according to the conditions of water, earth, fire, and air. So is a wave as a changed figure of the sea separate from the sea? No. There is no change in the fundamental, except between the calm and the surface ripples. Is there any real difference between the universe with no living things—the calm sea—and the one with manifested phenomena? It is the same whatever the shapes within it are like.

Then what is the cycle of rebirth? For example, a wave that

rises and falls for a moment might cause a passing boat to be hit and broken. Imagine saying, "You, a wave, how dare you strike and break the boat? Since you committed this sin you shall be reborn as a piece of dirt, according to your own deed." What an absurd way of thinking! This attitude adds individuality to a wave. Did the wave want to hit the boat?

There was once a big earthquake in Taiwan and many people died. Was it possible to say, "You, Earth, dared to make an earthquake and kill hundreds of innocent people? You must go to Hell and suffer punishment"? No. Why? Because there is no individual identity in the Earth. However, Earth caused this tragedy even though it has no individuality. There have been many typhoons that have swept whole towns away. Should we say, "You, typhoon, have been caught fair and square. You must go to Hell." Obviously the typhoon has killed or made homeless all the people in a town, but will it go to Hell? A human being would have to go to Hell for destroying a town; why not the typhoon? This highlights how absurd the idea of rebirth is—it comes from viewing humans as individual entities. It is ignorance, like viewing one cell of our bodies as an individual. There can be no such a thing.

What is it that makes up the cells in our bodies? The food we eat changes into nutrition and then becomes cells or energy. The need for food is another aspect of living things. Buddhism and some other groups teach not to kill living things. But no killing will result in no food, because plants and animals are all living things. There are so many living things, even in a glass of water. You can see them through a microscope despite invisibility to the naked eye. But if you say, "Do not kill living things," that means you cannot consume any other living things, and as a result you will die. Nevertheless these Buddhist monks who teach not to kill still eat food and live well. They only think animals should not be killed. The concept of life is limited to animals. Therefore Buddhists do not eat animals and eat only plants. Are the plants not living? Living things have to eat other living things to sustain their lives. That is a fact.

In short, if we eat beef, then the cow will come into our bodies to become cells and energy. What has the cow been changed into? It was changed into part of a human. A human ate the beef to gain nutrition to make new cells and get energy. As a result the cow has become human.

This, then, is the cycle of rebirth. As the cow becomes human and the human becomes maggots, everything turns around and around. If a human dies and is buried in the earth, worms eat away the body. When human dung is used as fertilizer, then the plants will eventually be eaten by humans. This is a condition of life, a symbiotic relationship in an endless cycle. If there is rebirth in the universe, this is it.

There is, however, no individual entity in the cycle of rebirth; all these objects are one. What spirits could come and go? Individual objects come to an end at their death. The body and the spirit disappear together. In this cycle there must be a principle; that is, the scientific energy-mass conservation law. Even though the cow disappeared, it transformed into other living things, whether it was eaten by worms or humans. From the perspective of total mass, there would, therefore, be no change although the cow has disappeared. That is the same in both science and the nature of the truth.

In truth there is no change overall. There is only universal rotation. It doesn't matter whether its shape is human or dog or worms or any other thing. All forms are turning within it. What is the difference whether a cell is a liver cell, intestinal cell, or anus cell in our bodies? Are all not "I"? In the universe there exists the energy-mass conservation law, which stipulates that there is no increase or decrease in energy. Even someone who is dead is not truly dead. What are they if not dead? Changed. But why do people say someone is dead when in reality they are merely changed? Why does such a notion arise? Because humans have mistakenly understood themselves as a subject with their own independent existence: I am dead. But "I" cannot be dead but only transformed.

Though the truth does not change, the manifested world will change. When you take a walk in a cemetery, you can see the grass growing and flowers on the graves. The plants grow by absorbing the nutrition from the bodies in the graves. All things change like this. The manifested world is constantly changing. The dead are changed but not really dead. The reason why people cling to life is fear of death. Why be afraid of death? Because it is misunderstood.

Scientists say that this universe will disappear after twenty-five billion years. And before that happens, in five billion years, so will Earth. That means Earth will disappear before the universe does. When Earth disappears, what will become of the people on it? Humanity needs to prepare to move to another planet.

How will Earth disappear? The sun will expand and then all planets around it will be absorbed into it. Then humans born on Earth and living on it as a cell shall disappear with it. The whole and the part are one. There is an incredible difference between cognizing the whole as one and cognizing only an individual identity. One who can view the whole as one does not insist on an individual as "I," because everything keeps changing and being replaced. When viewed from the perspective of the universe, is it sad that a human is dead, disappeared? There is no reason for sadness. It would, however, be sad if there were individual consciousness. Because the manifested appearance seems to be dead, it should be sad; however, there is no death. Then is anyone born? There is also no one who was born. There is no birth.

The whole just keeps changing, replacing its shape; this will be that, that will be this. The human consciousness makes fun out of the process of change, creating various events.

It is as if consciousness itself is writing a novel.

Who made the manifested universe? It comes from consciousness. Consciousness made the universe and then became deceived by itself. However, through the process, the consciousness can someday become enlightened.

Therefore, this universe can be said to be a one-man show of consciousness.

The Secret of Time and Space

Questions about the dimensionality of space-time are constantly arising, along with vague theories about the mysterious phenomena interlinked with it. Humanity has been wandering in delusion without seeing the truth—this comes from not fully understanding the concept of space-time.

Partly we can understand the questions of the universe scientifically, but there is another part that we cannot. We have already mentioned the part that it is possible to understand scientifically, so now let us talk about the other, hidden part.

<#1>

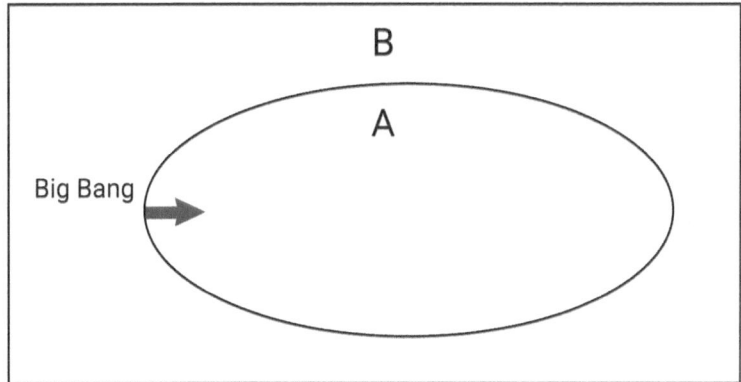

Modern science discovered that the universe is gradually expanding after the Big Bang. Which area marked A or B in the picture is the concept of space?

A is inside of the universe, expanding, and B is outside of the universe. In science A is called space and B is not said to be anything, because A is cognizable and B is not. But when we think deeply, how can A, the universe, be expanding without B?

Nevertheless, B does not exist phenomenally, because B is the foundation of the universe but cannot exist in the manifested world due to not being cognizable. It is true nature, the Absolute, the true "I" that cannot be conceptualized due to being out of cognition, in spite of being the original source of the universe.

Then, what is space? It is a concept within the limit of cognition born with the universe. This concept does not exist originally but is a name given out of necessity. So when the necessity is over, the concept will also disappear automatically. The "space" that we cognize did not exist originally, but only after the moment the universe was born in the Big Bang. After Earth was manifested and cognizable, a name for this concept, "space," was therefore given. But the name "space" will not last forever but disappear automatically the moment Earth disappears. So, the concept does not have its own existence originally but was born from another. In other words, the concept cannot exist eternally and has to disappear.

Then what is the biggest concept? That is the universe. The universe is the largest mass of functioning of birth and death. If the universe is a concept, what are all the existences in the universe? They all are also concepts. If not, what are they?

Next, let us study time. Generally, we conceive time as a linear flow through space.

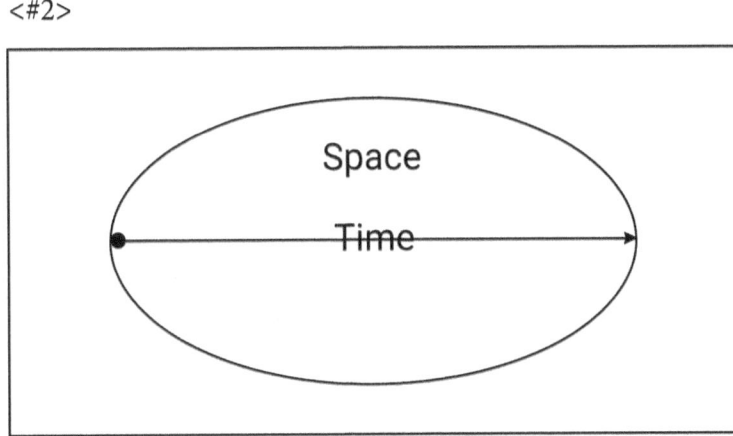

Now the standard of time is the speed of light. Modern science came to know the age and the size of the universe only after discovering the theory of the Big Bang. The age and the size of the universe are connected, because the moment the universe was born, time began, and the universe is expanding. Modern science says that the universe is 15 billion years old and has been expanding that whole time. It is, therefore, certainly a concept that time starts with the birth of the universe and will disappear with its death.

Another important fact is the relation between time and space. Many people understand mistakenly that time and space are separate, independent concepts. But they are concepts of relativity that cannot exist separately from each other, like the two sides of a coin. There can be neither time without space, nor vice versa. Time and space are therefore concepts of paired birth and death, appearing in a pair and disappearing in a pair along with the universe, the relative manifested world.

Another delusion people have is to think of both time and space as reality. But they are only the concepts cognizable during the existence of the universe, not the absolute realities.

Then let's look at why the concept of space-time is necessary for the universe to exist. We can discuss the existence of all beings, including the universe, only when they are cognizable. In order for an existing entity to be cognized, the concept of space to contain it is necessary due to being a volume of fixed size. Being revealed as a volume of fixed size can be cognized while it lasts for the duration of a fixed time, so the concept of time is necessary as well. Therefore, time and space must be conceptualized simultaneously, whether in relation to a material thing, a phenomenon, language or thought.

In summary, space-time is a concept that has to be born and die together with the universe. In order to cognize the universe and all beings in it, we need an aid—this is the concept of time-space. Time and space are easily misunderstood as independent concepts, but they are a dependent pair because they have to exist simultaneously in order to be cognized.

It is hard to understand the truth that the principle of relativity as the law of the manifested universe is a pair of concepts and functions in simultaneity, because people are restricted by divided individual consciousness.

Now let us go back to picture #2; first, from the standpoint of time:

"Before the Big Bang" is understood to be a state of nothingness. Because the concepts of time and space began after the Big Bang, there can be said to be a state of "is-ness" when it is possible to cognize a phenomenon using time and space.

Second, from the standpoint of space:

"Outside the space that has been expanding after the Big Bang" from the scientific perspective can only be nothingness, because the concept of space-time cannot be applied. In other words, only the manifested universe can be considered as a state of is-ness because it is cognizable by the concept of space-time.

From the standpoint of science this logic is undeniable. But it is not such an easy question from the standpoint of philosophy. If there is really nothing "before" the Big Bang or outside the universe, upon what basis was the universe born, and how could it keep expanding? Therefore, "time" before the Big Bang and "outside" the space of the universe are simply incognizable, but surely exist. Therefore we call it the absolute emptiness beyond the limit of cognition, and Sakyamuni Buddha called it true nature.

Modern science discovered that the universe as believed to be unlimited in space and permanent in time is just a concept of a phenomenon in fact limited in space and time. Though humanity tried to find the everlasting and unlimited truth, they could not, because the permanent and unlimited true nature is the Absolute, beyond the range of relative cognition system. People have tried to understand true nature with relative cognition and so it cannot but be distorted.

Before the Big Bang has to be expressed as "nothingness"

because nothing is incognizable in the phenomenal world. And people understand the Absolute as nothingness or emptiness due to viewing it as a state of disconnection from relative cognition. But because there is not even a concept of is-ness and nothingness, form and emptiness, there cannot be such discrimination in time before or after the Big Bang and inside or outside the universe. Therefore, if we view the nothingness (*mu*) of the pre-Big Bang or the emptiness (*gong*) of outside the universe as true nature, it would be like falling into dualistic discrimination.

There is no limitation of time and space in the Absolute. The Absolute should always be itself before and after the birth and death of the universe. On the basis of true nature, the Absolute, the universe of manifested phenomena appears or disappears, but nevertheless true nature itself is not changed. Birth-death, before-after, and inside-outside exist only in the universe, limited by space-time but there is no limitation in the Absolute itself. Therefore, the manifested world will not be eternal or unlimited—only the Absolute, true nature, will be thus.

Then let us talk about how people recognize time and space in the manifested universe. Time is seen in one dimension due to being cognized as a flow in one direction, to the future. Space is cognized as three dimensions due to its consisting of three dimensions of front-back, left-right and up-down. Recently, through remarkable developments in quantum mechanics, the universe has been discovered to have had eleven dimensions originally, but after the Big Bang only four dimensions were manifested through expansion, with the others hidden from our perception. Therefore, we cannot cognize the dimensions outside our own four dimensions; that is a limitation of human cognition.

Humanity had believed that the absolute time of one dimension and the absolute space of three dimensions existed as independent realities until the publication of Einstein's theory of relativity. However, in 1905, Einstein announced the theory of relativity: the universe was discovered to be four dimensions of space-time because time and space could not be separated as independent concepts from each other.

It is, however, still a problem that human consciousness cognizes time as a one-dimensional flow of the past, present, and future, and space as a separate reality such as front-back, left-right, up-down, and here-there, even 100 years after the announcement of the theory of relativity. Furthermore, religious believers or mystics call the invisible world the fourth dimension and name it the spiritual world, Heaven, life after death, outside of the universe etc. People come to believe in those dimensions because there are many who even say that they have been in or seen such worlds. But they are deluded by their own consciousness. They understand it mistakenly as real experience that they see various manifestations, as if the consciousness dreams. It is also deception by the consciousness to experience a past life by hypnosis, popular in modern days.

Ninety-nine percent of spiritual experiences that people have believed for thousands of years until now are nothing but a comedy that sprang from the delusion about phenomena believed blindly. But there is one percent of truth hidden that has to be recognized as reality. Therefore people are confused. For example, some people guess correctly events of the past or the future without any pre-knowledge or any relationship with them, or what is happening at a place thousands of miles away. We call such a person a prophet, clairvoyant, medium, or psychic. Not everything they experience is true. However, if there is even one percent of truth in their experiences, they should not be ignored. It is this one percent of truth that we are going to explain.

There have been several remarkable prophets throughout history, within and without the sphere of religion. Among them are typical prophets, like Nostradamus of the European Middle Ages, Edgar Cayce, the "sleeping clairvoyant" in the USA, and in Korea, Namsago of the Choseon Dynasty and the Jeong-gamrok prophecies by an unknown writer. There have been many other prophets worldwide.

Though people are filled with admiration that over ninety-nine percent of major prophecies have come true, they actually remain unable to see the truth in them. If a prophecy told one hundred years ago has come true, what does it mean?

People are shocked by the supernatural power of the predictor, but the real importance is not so superficial. The fact that someone saw an incident happen one hundred years later means that everything has already been decided. The reason why people cannot accept such a plain and simple truth is their belief that they make decisions and behave with their own free will. There cannot be free will because the universe is the manifested world based on the theory of relativity. My thoughts, words, and behaviors are from the common decisions of two-way communication with partners. Since the whole universe, not only human relations, is connected, these actions are flowing correctly according to an ordained scenario.

Then what is the range of that which is ordained? There is ordination from the birth to the death of a life, on a small scale, and the appearing and disappearing of the universe at a greater level. All beings have already been preordained, but humans understand mistakenly that all their thoughts, words, and actions are accomplished every time by their own judgment and decision.

How can prophets see the future, when other people can't? To resolve this question, we have to know the secret of the concept of space-time.

The universe as cognized by humans has four dimensions: three dimensions of space plus one dimension of time.

But we cannot see four dimensions totally in the beta wave state of usual consciousness, but see only partial time and partial space; while we stay here in space, we cannot cognize it completely. However, if we are able to connect to the alpha or theta wave states through meditation or religious practice, the cognition of reality will stop and cognition that jumps over the limit of space-time will open up to us. Through changes in the brainwaves, the perception of reality during sleep will stop and be replaced with dreaming a state of non-reality. Thus we come to experience strongly non-realistic phenomena usually impossible to see.

But these experiences will rise to the surface of the consciousness under the influence of a fixed idea from deep in the subconscious. For example, Christians may experience seeing Heaven or Hell or meeting Jesus, while Buddhists might meet Buddha or Bodhisattva or an ancestor in the land of ultimate bliss. There are many other people who see aliens or ghosts or a past life. They are not lying. They come to believe due to having strong experiences. Their experiences, however, are not all true, even though they did experience them directly, because fixed ideas springing from wrong information in the subconscious continuously distort the consciousness without them knowing.

In other words, they come to have experiences that follow the direction of their beliefs. Christians do not meet Buddha and Buddhists do not meet Jesus. People who believe in rebirth can see their past lives and those who don't cannot. Though a person can have spiritual experiences in a state of alpha or theta wave during meditation or dreams, over ninety-nine percent of it is not pure.

Only an experience in pure consciousness, free from distorted, deeply fixed ideas, free from the bondage of here-there, limits of space and the past-present-future of time, is the truth. In that state of consciousness are all the dimensions of time and space functioning as simultaneity. It is, therefore, possible when past, present and future disappear and only spontaneity functions that we can see an incident that will happen in one hundred years' time.

And it is also possible when space, here and there, is unlimited and cognized as spontaneity that we can see an incident happening at a place thousands of miles away. How is it possible for such things to happen? Because there is fundamentally no such dimension of time and space in the Absolute, the truth. The concept of space-time was necessarily introduced to cognize the materials manifested in the process of the birth of the universe.

Time and space did not originally exist. If we cognize time only as the linear stream of past, present and future, then it will become a fixed idea that will stop us from knowing the spontaneity of time-space.

There is fundamentally no time and space. Therefore all the incidents happening in the manifested universe are a mere dream.

Dependent Origination with No-self and Individual Rebirth

The main teaching of Buddhism is the three Dharma characteristics: impermanence, suffering, and no-self. Of these, impermanence and suffering are preparation stages for realizing the no-self. So the three Dharma characteristics are concluded in no-self. If you naturally understand impermanence and suffering in the process of an awareness practice to realize no-self, realization of no-self comes naturally.

Buddha had a saying about impermanence, suffering, and no-self in the Nikaya sutra:

"Sona, what do you think about whether materials change or not?"

"They have to change."

"If they have to change, is it suffering or pleasure?"

"It is suffering."

Changing means impermanence. Impermanence means not everlasting, perpetual change. All materials and lives in the manifested universe are continuously changing.

"If they are subject to change, is it suffering or pleasure?" It is, of course, suffering, because they cannot exist as they are but keep changing. That is suffering because all materials are changing. If there is suffering due to change, it means that there is not suffering when there is no changing. What is no-suffering? It is no-changing, and no-changing is true nature, the Absolute, it is everlasting.

Buddha explained no-self, the third characteristic, as follows:

"If changing is suffering, can we say, 'this is me, this is mine, this is my nature'?"

"No, we cannot say so."

"Can we say that the one that is impermanent and suffering is 'I' as the subject?"

"No, we cannot say so."

If we cannot say it is "I," then what is it? It is no-self, due to not being me. According to this syllogism, all sentient beings in the phenomenal universe are impermanent, they are suffering due to impermanence, and because they are not permanent and are suffering, they have no-self. In conclusion, there is no-self, but Buddha explained impermanence and suffering as means in order to teach no-self.

It is, therefore, one Dharma characteristic, rather than three, because the truth is only no-self. Impermanence and suffering are just means of explaining no-self.

Mahayana Buddhism replaces suffering with nirvana: the three Dharma characteristics therefore consist of impermanence, nirvana, and no-self. Some Buddhists claim four dharmas, adding nirvana instead of replacing suffering.

No-self is nirvana. No-self is not separate from nirvana. This is nothing but a play on words. All you have to do is to realize no-self.

No-self, no existence of *I*, means that there is no main character "I," just a subject unchanging within any living thing and all materials in the phenomenal universe. But Buddhism studies the five aggregations and twelve links of dependent origination, because those must be learned in order to realize the three Dharma characteristics. However, I did not know them when I reached enlightenment. Though I wrote them down while studying a long time ago, I cannot remember them now if asked. However, let us understand the five aggregations and twelve links of dependent origination, as, although these are not necessary for enlightenment, they are insisted on by Buddhists nowadays.

Five aggregations mean an existence consisting of five elements. An existence as a living thing is subject to birth-death. Existence is a combined construct of body and mind and again can be divided into five characteristics or aggregations: form, reception, conception, formation of the mind, and coming into consciousness. With form, the material, the body, and the functioning of the mind is divided into four steps. I was so surprised to hear that existence consists of five elements; I was full of admiration: "How can the mind be divided in four steps, in such detail?" However, after enlightenment, I came to know that such explanation of details is not useful but only makes people feel complicated. Simply speaking, existence is the combined organization of body and mind. Nevertheless, even the body and the mind are not two but one. It is consciousness that causes the body and the mind to be cognized separately. When the pure consciousness manifests itself into the relative world, it is impossible for one concept to be cognized and so appears as relative concepts.

The body is yin-body and the mind is yang-body. That means one is divided and projected into two. It is, however, mistakenly understood that the body and mind are separated due to these concepts, but the body-mind is not two but one. The body follows where the mind goes. But the mind changes so rapidly that it cannot be totally projected into the body. Therefore people are deluded that the body and the mind are separate beings. Some disciples say, "Though I am eager to go to the meditation center, I am very busy and so cannot go," but this is not possible. If the mind is keen enough, then the body will move that way by itself.

Actually the mind is not eager but indecisive. Therefore it tends to move to the stronger side. The mind is ever-changing, and while it is confused about what to do, you will go where it is more attracted. So even if you are thinking about other options, those will not be better than where the body goes.

We have to know the characteristics of the mind. The body-mind is projected by consciousness. To manifest the body-mind, they must be manifested as relative, because they have to be cognized. This is very important. It seems, therefore, that one must be divided into two—birth in pairs. In fact, it is not two that appears but one, and this appearance is manifested as one but features two characteristics—birth in pairs. It feels like a separated appearance because of the dualistic world. We tend to see the division because the phenomenal world is made by separated consciousness, though it is fundamentally one existence.

Why does the separated consciousness appear? Because of relativity. The phenomenal world necessarily has divided consciousness. No being in the phenomenal world can escape it. The enlightened one also sees in divided consciousness—see this as *I* and that as *you* in common with an unenlightened person. The enlightened one is not confused by this, but the unenlightened one sees this as *I* and that as *you* as existing in reality. The enlightened one does not confuse the oneness even when it is divided into this-that or I-you as concepts, illusionary entities projected to manifest themselves. When manifested in the phenomenal world, one becomes divided into I-you. However, when free from dualistic discrimination, there is just one and the divided consciousness cannot work anymore.

In the Absolute, this divided consciousness cannot work. If we stand in the center of pure consciousness, we are in pure consciousness while cognizing the divided consciousness. While we exist as an apparent individual, we know that the true nature is one. Every individual is seen as one simultaneously. However, the unenlightened sees only with divided consciousness, forgetting completely the pure consciousness as a fundamental basis for everything.

Forgetting the pure consciousness, they see only the divided and visible objects. Simply speaking, the enlightened one sees the sea with waves as the whole sea, as one; that is, while cognizing the whole sea, he sees the waves of the sea as they are. They never forget to cognize the one sea as a whole whether there are waves on it or not. But the unenlightened one identifies themself with the waves that come and go, as if one wave thinks of another one as *you*. However, the enlightened person is not in the wave-consciousness but in the sea-consciousness as a whole. That is pure consciousness. They are not deluded by the divided consciousness, but also cognize manifested beings as they are. They see the waves as they rise and fall. Both the enlightened and the unenlightened are alike in the way they see; however, the enlightened one in pure consciousness never forgets the fundamental truth that the entire manifested world undergoes the continuous cycle of birth-death by dependent origination.

Ego is not sea-consciousness but wave-consciousness. In a split second a person can become wave-consciousness, thinking of the wave appearing and disappearing within a second as "I" without seeing the whole. But the wave is an illusion that appears and disappears rapidly. It is an ignorant sentient being who clings to the thought of the wave as "I" in spite of this illusion.

Now let us talk about the twelve dependent originations. Buddha realized no-self and dependent origination. The two are not different; no-self is dependent origination and vice versa. Do not think of them as separate. Dependent origination means that when A exists, B can be born; A makes B, B makes C, and C makes D, and likewise sequentially. Dependent origination exists as relativity but cannot be alone, because one cannot cognize oneself without another. Cognition requires the seer and the seen and so there have to be two at least. Therefore the manifested exist in relativity. No existence can be born by itself and nothing can exist alone.

This is the principle of dependent origination. There is, therefore, no-self as subjectivity in all existences. No-self and dependent origination are one. Buddha explained dependent origination very simply like this: "If this appears, that also appears, and if this disappears, that also disappears." But some brilliant people broke down dependent origination into twelve links of causational arising.

These are: (1) ignorance (2) formation (3) consciousness (4) name-form (5) the six organs (6) contact (7) sensation (8) desire (9) grasping (10) being (11) birth (12) old/dead. Ignorance is the fundamental cause by which all beings are born and therefore dependent origination begins. Fundamental ignorance follows conception; good and bad karma by physical and spiritual activities, which is claimed to be the cause of rebirth. Next follows consciousness, in which all good and bad karma for life are memorized.

Name-form means that reception, thought, formation, and consciousness become a subject of rebirth to change the body, and be memorized within it to be connected to the next life. Due to fundamental ignorance, good and bad karma are made and memorized and then the body will be born according to that memory. That is form.

The six organs are eyes, ears, nose, tongue, body, and volition. "Contact" means that when the six organs interact with objects they become the six consciousnesses. "Sensation" means three senses: suffering, pleasure and no-suffering, and no-pleasure from the six consciousnesses. "Desire" means that when material things appear, there also come like-dislike feelings related to them. "Grasping" is the attachment that wishes to grasp good things and discard bad ones. "Being" means existence. The karma from the accumulated existence—"what I am"—is fixed here to give birth in the next life. Birth will occur again through the cycle of birth-death. Old and dead means to get old and die because you have been born. If you are not enlightened, you must rotate by the principle of these 12 links of causation.

Then what is the key point of the 12 links of causation? In conclusion, I am born, I commit sin, I die, I am judged, and I am reborn. That is the claim not of dependent origination with no-self, but individual rebirth.

The true nature, *I*, is no birth-death, so then who is reborn? Some say that enlightenment comes from mastering the five aggregations and twelve links of causation. The core element of twelve links of causation is rebirth, which rotates in this cycle. Maybe there are many more than twelve because the mind changes so fast. We have to just recognize the efforts involved in such detailed classification.

Likewise, when we fully understand the five aggregations and the twelve links of causation, it is said that we can realize no-permanence, suffering, and no-self. However, I realized these three Dharma characteristics without even knowing what they were. If I had studied and discussed those things, then I could not be enlightened. That is the reason why many Buddhist monks have not been enlightened even though they have practiced so much.

There were also many stages laid out on the way to enlightenment: Su-da-won, Sah-dah-ham, Ah-nah-ham, Arahat, Sravaka, Pratyekabuddha, Bodhisattva, and Buddha.

In fact, if you go to Myanmar, you can see many monks and laypeople in temples who wish to become Su-da-won at least, not even hoping to become Arahat. The reason for this is that if they can get into the Su-da-won stage, they can become Buddha in the seventh rebirth. It is said to be destined. They say that even if they attain Su-da-won and then there is no practice, they can be enlightened to become Buddha in the seventh life. So they wish to become Su-da-won, the first stage of the Arahat, at least. They want a guarantee that they will become Buddha. It is the result from the delusion of thinking "I" is born, will die some day, and be reborn continuously by karma.

There have been many strange doctrines added in both northern and southern Buddhism over the last 2,500 years. What remains is only blind belief in Buddhism.

I too was deluded by it. When I went to Myanmar for the first time, I thought that I wished to become Su-da-won at least. The nature of everybody's ego is not so different. And I was at a loss until I became enlightened. I was nearly driven mad, because something seemed to be within my grasp but could not be. Likewise, many truth-seekers are suffering inside. While they are practicing hard and suffering for enlightenment, such additional doctrines make them become more ignorant.

It is said that there are two obstacles to being enlightened:

defilement and the known. Defilements arise from delusion and the thought of identifying the body with *I*, the ego, causing suffering. The obstacle of the known hinges on what seems to be real. If people's heads are full of the wrong views and religious doctrines, those are obstacles to enlightenment.

In fact, Buddhism itself is stuck at these two obstacles. Buddhists speak about rebirth, but who is reborn? While they are suffering from delusion from the false *I*, ego, such belief in rebirth will make their ego stronger, so that more defilements shall emerge. Next, the obstacle of the known creates such absurd and wrong doctrines to brainwash people, making them grow away from the truth. However, while Buddhism itself is doing this, it is saying not to do it; what a comedy it is! There are so many things like this.

Buddhism and Hinduism, India's traditional religions, have influenced each other. The six rebirths is a concept from Hinduism. "No-self and dependent origination," realized by Buddha 2,500 years ago, were to reform the theory of rebirth espoused in Hinduism.

This dependent origination with no-self means no rebirth. There is no-self in all beings, so who is reborn? True *I* is original nature. This is no-self. Therefore to become no-self means to become the true *I*—not *I* existing as an individual entity, only *I* as wholeness, oneness. That is the true *I*. No-self as spoken of by Buddha equals true *I*, as spoken by Maharshi or Maharaj.

The concept of rebirth had existed for 3000 years when Buddha broke it down. Buddha was born and lived in India, and studied the Veda at first. Moreover, he studied it through great teachers and so came to believe in that concept of rebirth. However, when he was enlightened under a bodhi tree after practicing very hard for six years, he realized dependent origination and no-self. Buddha overturned the concept of rebirth at that time. But today, Buddhism has returned to its former state. Now Buddhism talks about rebirth again. It is ridiculous that Buddhists both admit dependent origination with no-self and also talk about rebirth.

When they are asked, "What is no-self?", then they say, "There is no I." And when they are asked, "Then what is rebirth?" they say, "Sentient beings unenlightened are reborn continuously by their own karma." Isn't it strange that they say "no-self" here and "rebirth by karma" there?

Moreover, they say that they are reborn in six realms: underworld, hungry ghost, animal, suffering being, human, and upper world.

The world after death can be roughly categorized into two; a linear point of view and a circular point of view. This linear point of view means that sentient beings are born and live, and the bodies disappear while the spirits move to Heaven or Hell to live forever. Christianity is the most representative example. On the other hand, the circular point of view means continuous revolution—Buddhism and Hinduism are in that category. But Hinduism had the linear point of view at first; therefore the circular point of view can be said to be a more evolved state than the linear one.

However, Christianity kept insisting on the linear point of view, while on the other hand, wise people in India began to insist on rebirth instead of the Heaven-Hell concept. More evolved consciousnesses spoke about rebirth. However, Buddha realized that all beings are subject to dependent origination. The cycle of rebirth equals the dependent origination, but people recognize rebirth as individual due to their delusions. Dependent origination cannot literally assume individuality. It is dependent origination in which the whole revolves as oneness, the cycle of rebirth applying to the whole.

We must not misunderstand the concept of rebirth. From the viewpoint of an ego, it means that the individual entity repeats birth-death constantly, while from the viewpoint of the whole, when an individual appears and disappears, then another individual appears. It is the rebirth of dependent origination because of the rotation of all phenomena, but it becomes individual rebirth because of being perceived from the viewpoint of ego. It is therefore ignorance, as when people see only the finger pointing at the moon, not the moon itself. It is so sad that people accept this on their own terms even when the enlightened teach the truth. When the enlightened person says "I," it means the true *I*, while unenlightened beings think it is I, an individual. Likewise the same *I* comes to be accepted by each differently. Why is the speaker so different from the listener? Because of delusions. Then who is deluded?

The subject that is deluded is consciousness. Who made the body-mind? Consciousness did. When the Absolute manifests itself into the phenomenal world, it must be done through consciousness. Consciousness, as the subject of cognition, projected the body-mind; that means it made the manifested universe. Who is it that identifies one point in the phenomenal universe with "I"? It is consciousness. Who is suffering under that delusion? It is also consciousness. Later the enlightenment will also be through consciousness. Therefore, consciousness is doing a one-man show. There is fundamentally no individual consciousness. So we must not say "individual consciousness." It is just consciousness.

But while the manifested consciousness had evolved, its limitation has changed. A long time ago, the thought of the afterlife was only from the linear point of view, then later wiser people said, "No, the spirit after death shall rotate," and claimed the circular point of view. However, the enlightened one realizes that there is rebirth not as an individual entity, but within the whole as one. That is dependent origination with no-self. Therefore rebirth is dependent with no-self. But from the viewpoint of ego, it is mistakenly understood that the self, I, shall rotate. Therefore Buddhism teaches about the twelve links of causation and the rebirth in six stages.

There is a difference between Christianity and Buddhism; in Christianity the spirit will stay forever in Heaven or Hell after death, but in Buddhism, even if the spirit goes to Hell, it can go to better places, and though it lives as a human, it can fall to being an animal if it does bad things. In Christianity there is only a fixed afterlife, but in Buddhism there is a possibility of a changed afterlife. From such a perspective, the afterlife of Buddhism can be said to have a wider range than that of Christianity.

However, there is no difference between them from the perspective of egoistic ideas. It is like they are writing a varied and interesting novel with the character "I" originally not existing; going to Hell and emerging to go to Heaven. If they believe in Buddha, they can go to the pure land where Buddha stays. With a false *I* they are writing a novel. Therefore, if we look into Buddhism a little more carefully, we see that Buddhism falls into a state of coma.

Today, the reason why religions are confusing is because of the limitation of consciousness. Let us look at the word "God," used in Christianity. Christians use God as the Absolute being, like a personality. This word is used for people too. If the Absolute is expressed as a personality, an individual being, it is not the Absolute anymore. It is a relative being. If not enlightened, people could confuse the Absolute with the relative. Where is God as the Absolute being? The Absolute is just the Absolute.

The Absolute cannot appear as one being and be named. But ignorant people made the Absolute into an individual entity. Saying, "Buddha appears all around the manifested world" means that all beings are essentially Buddha in the perspective of the original nature, the Absolute; stone, tree and everything else. True nature is like this. All are truth. All are Buddha, truth itself. However, if you see it with the wrong viewpoint, then it will be the same as Christianity. If you see Buddha as an individual, all can be confused. In the Lotus Sutra Buddha changes into a magician.

But if you understand that sutra more correctly, it is not a groundless story. It is based on the truth. Buddha, true nature, can manifest all around the phenomenal universe. This is because the phenomenal universe was projected from true nature itself. Therefore Buddha can appear all over the pure land. That saying is right from the perspective of the truth. But if Buddha is expressed as a personality, it is wrong. Christianity is also saying, "Father God is the Absolute, omniscient, omnipotent, and omnipresent." So what then is the meaning of that?

When God exists as an individual, is it not possible that God is not everywhere? That saying itself already means that the whole is God. It means the Absolute. Yet while saying so, Christians are again making an individual of God, the Absolute.

Buddhists use the expression "the pure land where Amida Buddha stays." What is the result? Buddha becomes an individual. They are saying these words mindlessly. God living in Heaven in Christianity and Amida Buddha staying in the pure land in Buddhism are the same. There is not much difference between the two.

If they do not know the truth, then come ridiculous expressions due to the confusion between the Absolute and the relative. Buddha is not an individual. Because people view Gautama Buddha as an enlightened person, they view him as an individual. No-self is the concept that there is not "I" existing independently, so how could he be an individual? Individuality had already disappeared.

There is basically no individuality, but only consciousness, pure consciousness. But the unenlightened are in a state of individual consciousness and so view the enlightened and themselves through an individual consciousness in which they always stay. Even though Buddha realized no-self, they view the no-self as an enlightened individual. They believe Buddha also had that perspective. But more problematic, they view themselves as individuals. How wonderful if they could view all as true nature! They view all things as being the same individuals as themselves, not realizing that there is no self—they are not enlightened.

It is, therefore, a mindless saying even though they write greater scripture than Tripitaka Koreana in a state of not no-self. If there is not no-self within, every saying is untrue. It is just a ridiculous saying; a fiction. Their trying to make the fiction more interesting resulted in the three thousand worlds, the Amida world, and the Maitrea in Tusita-deva, etc. Such writings are just a novel about an imaginary world without any proof. The Tripitaka Koreana is just like a novel. The truth of all Buddhist scriptures is only one, no-self. The Mahayana scriptures were written 1000 years after Buddha's death. We should know that history.

In the beginning, after the death of Buddha Sakyamuni, the time of primitive Buddhism, only the Theravada scriptures had been written. Though there were some changes after many years, the concept of dependent origination with no-self was expressed in those scriptures. After that, there appeared concepts like Sudawon in southern Buddhism, while the Early Buddhist School appeared. It is said that Buddhist scriptures were passed to Myanmar and Thailand before Mahayana Buddhism, due to their location near India. Of course, after that there were people who distorted the truth in Theravada Buddhism, such as the venerable Nagarjuna, Mahayana Buddhist. Buddhist scriptures of Mahayana were much more distorted because they appeared after many years. Nevertheless, the main train of thought remains that of Buddha.

Though the fundamental thoughts of Buddha are in the three typical scriptures—the Flower Ornament Sutra, the Diamond Sutra, and the Lotus Sutra—most of the thoughts, concepts, and content of Buddhist writings were made many years later. Furthermore, ideas from Hinduism were mixed in among them. There are many gods in Hinduism. From those gods came the concept of Bodhisattva. Did Sakyamuni Buddha ever mention the Bodhisattva? No. When you are enlightened, all beings become true nature. So who can save whom?

It is the phenomenal world that true nature is manifested into. Buddha said after enlightenment, "I am free from birth and death." This means that he was never born in reality. This born body-mind is not reality because I am the true nature. The body-mind is not reality and so, who can save whom? Can a phantom save a phantom? Therefore Buddha said, "Life is a dream. This world is a dream. All are just a dream." Now people are living in a dream—how can they be saved?

How can we save a person who is suffering in a paralyzing nightmare? The only way is to wake them up; shake them awake. If there is salvation, it will make them enlightened.

It is, however, not enlightenment that they say is salvation in Buddhism and Christianity. It is said that if someone believes in Buddha, they can go to the pure land; if they believe in Jesus, they can go to Heaven. However, a dream will end by itself even without the dreamer being awoken. A dream starts by itself and also ends by itself.

There is, therefore, nothing that the enlightened can do with compassion. There is no person to be saved; how can compassion arise? Only when there is delusion that there are sentient beings to be saved, will compassion arise. This is the terrible delusion. Compassion arises only from the minds of deluded people.

Because of that there came the Kstigabha Bodhisattva saying, "I will never be enlightened until all sentient beings come out of the gate of Hell." Amazing! I respected the Kstigabha Bodhisattva very much before. But this seemed such a stupid saying after I was enlightened. There is nothing more than ego in it. Nowadays, Buddhism says this in order to further strengthen the Buddhists' beliefs.

Some 99.9 percent of Buddhist scriptures were written by blind Buddhists—just 0.1 percent of them are Buddha's true words.

The thought that there Buddha and sentient beings are separate is a dualistic discrimination by relative concepts. All beings are the result of the manifestation of the Absolute. It is, therefore, said that Buddha is not an individual entity. Sakyamuni, as a manifested individual, is a character in the play; an imaginary character in the novel. It is not for Sakyamuni to be enlightened. He performs a role as a Buddha character in the novel. What did Sakyamuni realize? In essence, there is not a real entity Sakyamuni. The role of Buddha was given to him: "You will perform a role as the enlightened in this play." Likewise Adolf Hitler was given a role: "You will perform a role as the killer in this play." Think of it—the name of the character Sakyamuni is true nature but so is that of Hitler. One true nature performs a role as Sakyamuni, as Hitler, as Gandhi, as Napoleon, and all the others. Therefore who shall be praised, who be humiliated, who be respected? The reality is one. So there is no identification and condemnation if you see the source of all manifestations as noumenon.

The killer is just a character in the play. Everyone can blame the character in the play. But after the play ends, nobody blames the person who played the role. Because that was just the play. However, if we mistakenly identified ourselves as existing independently, we will blame him even off-stage. If that happens, it is inevitable that Buddha and sentient beings exist separately, but they are all one if we do not misunderstand the fundamental truth. Though there is a difference in a role, the source is one.

For example, this body is one chunk. There are eyes, ears, and mouth in a chunk that perform different roles. It is the same in that, though they are in different roles, the whole body is still called "I." When we say "I," it means the whole body. We do not divide the body into trillions of cells to call *I* or *you*, but call the whole *I*. It is, therefore, *I* as the whole that we call *I*.

We never used the word *I* for those individuals, because we do not call one cell in the body *I*. While we call the whole *I* every day, *I* becomes an individual entity due to dualistic consciousness. Then, because the whole manifested universe is one body, we can perceive it as *I*. It means that we perceive the biggest, the universe, to be cognizable as *I* instead of a being confined in one body. Nevertheless, this phenomenal universe will also disappear in the end. Therefore it is not the true *I*. Even though you experienced cosmic consciousness, it is not truth. It is not true enlightenment. Even that experience is an illusion. It cannot, therefore, be enlightenment through an individual consciousness, as *I* experiences the universal as the biggest limitation. Only the experience of no-self is perfect enlightenment. However huge the individual entity is, there is no *I* as an individual in it. When you realize the true self as true nature, that is perfect enlightenment. Even the universal entity cannot be subject to birth and death when there is no limitation.

Distorted Words of Truth

Mu-wi-ja-yeon [Nature itself remained intact]

Even famous scholars do not know how to correctly interpret the word *mu* (nothing). Their interpretations of *mu-wi* (doing nothing) are completely wrong.

What is *mu-wi*? A more correct expression is *mu-wi-ja-yeon*.

It means nature itself has remained intact. People usually interpret the phrase as "to go back to nature itself." For example, people say, "Why is humanity suffering in this complicated and polluted world? Because they are living by *in-wi* [human work, artificiality], not by *mu-wi*. They have to go back to nature." But this thought is very wrong. *Mu-wi-ja-yeon* means that the truth is as it is. If people interpret it wrongly, they think there is *mu-wi-ja-yeon* and an artificial culture as an opposite concept, or a state of not being that way psychologically. In other words, nature is as it is, but it becomes a culture if people build a house within nature, because the house is built by human activity. It is said by philosophers, religious people, and many others that this world will disappear soon because people live not by the laws of nature, but by destroying nature with human activity.

Therefore they should go back to nature itself in order to save humanity.

But let us think about why that expression is wrong. When we say, "Let us go back to nature itself as it remains intact," what is the action of going back? That in itself is human activity.

"Nature itself remains intact" actually means that truth itself is as it is. If people destroy a mountain to build a road, what is this? It is also *mu-wi-ja-yeon*. It is all the more problematic to make a dualistic discrimination of this as artificial activity. If things happen here and now, it is truth. Where should we go back to? Because of dualistic discrimination and the fixed standpoint of good and evil, people think human activity is wrong. There is nothing wrong about it. *Mu-wi-ja-yeon* means that the relative world at present is truth as it is. The state of flowing naturally is a law of nature. It is truth, a law of nature even if things do not seem good, i.e. even though it doesn't feel good that there is global warming, it is truth. Though there are so many evil people in this world, that also is truth and a law of nature. Even though Earth is being destroyed, that is truth. Because Earth was born, it is subject to being destroyed in the end. But people do not like death, only birth. They think that to save life is truth but to take life is not. However, the truth is not so narrow-minded. All things are truth whether it is killing or saving lives. All manifestations in the universe are truth.

Not only religious people but ordinary folk often say, "Let us live according to the laws of nature." What does this mean? "The laws of nature;" the term itself is the law of nature. But why would someone add the words, "let us live" to that? This is *in-wi* (human work). As such, to live in the laws of nature" necessitates some human action. But the phrase, the law of nature, does not refer to human work but that which is. Therefore letting things go on is the law of nature. Nevertheless, people say, "Why do you live like this? Live by the law of nature." This expression makes the truth into human work. All manifestations in the phenomenal universe are living as their own roles were assigned, by the laws of nature.

When explaining the laws of nature, water is often given as an example. Water flows, going around the stone ahead, waiting in front of a bank and going again when there is enough to overflow. In this case, does the water go around the stone of its own free will? No, it flows around automatically. It does not have free will. When blocked by a dam, is the water patient and waiting? When overflowing the dam, is the water going over it through its own effort and shouting, "I am going over"? No. The water staying in the pond will become stagnant. That is the law of nature.

The law of nature is as it is. If we live like this, like that, it is human activity and so the word itself is a contradiction. Even though it might not be satisfactory to me, the law of nature is the law of nature; it is the truth that your husband is cheating on you, due to the scenario he has been given in the play. It is the law of nature, *mu-wi-ja-yeon*, that people fight with each other, or that others try to get them not to fight. All events are being played according to the scenario that comes from dependent origination.

If we accept that all things are the law of nature whether

they are good or bad, there will be no suffering, but ego cannot accept it and so we feel hurt and sad. But the one who injured me was simply accomplishing the role assigned to him.

The play is a kind of game in which there are no real characters and real events. If they themselves organize the game to get hurt and suffer by it, it is a stupid thing to do. A game is a game. The cause of all such suffering is the delusion mistakenly identifying "I" with the body-mind. From this emerges concepts of me, my family, my nation, and attachment and suffering follow. However, if enlightened, such concepts do not exist any longer because the delusion, the ego, disappears; there is no thought of even me and my family. Apparently there are family members as characters; husband, wife, and children. However, there is no such family as "mine" as people think. They are just playing their roles as characters.

Nor is there dualistic discrimination in anything happening inside or outside, because all things are going by the law of nature according to the scenario. The enlightened one, merged into the truth, not an individual entity, is carrying out their role as given by the dependent origination principle. However, if we forget true nature, wholeness, and are shut in the limits of individuality, we experience dualistic discrimination, clinging to our selves or feeling desire or suffering when we are not satisfied. But we do not need to do this if we realize the truth. If we see the manifested universe, the delusion, as it is, without dualistic discrimination, then it is completeness, the truth and the law of nature itself. This is *mu-wi-ja-yeon* (nature itself remaining intact).

Mu-wi-ja-yeon is to view things as they are.

No-Mind

If you wrongly interpret the term *mu-shim* (no-mind), it becomes "there is no mind." There was, however, originally no such meaning. This state can be possible only when it becomes no-self. No-self is no-mind. When there is no-self, whatever arises in the mind are the concepts of nothing. No-mind is different from no-interest (indifference). Mind is divided into both interest and no-interest. Interest is to have a mind on something or someone, but no-interest is not to do so. So an interest is to keep thinking about something even after leaving it. No-interest means not to pay any attention to others even when together, as well as after leaving them. But no-mind means no-self-mind, in a word. Then what is "doing [something] with no-mind"?

Even if there are some people who act with no-mind, this is very wrong. How can you do something without mind? Action means to follow a thought when it arises in the mind. Therefore, doing something with no-mind doesn't mean acting without mind, but acting with no-self. Doing with no-self means doing without me doing the acting. It becomes doing with no-mind only when there is no "I" who acts. Simply speaking, doing with no-self is doing with no-mind. There is a big difference between being "no-I who acts" and "not my action." Being "no-I who acts" means that there is an action but no "I" who makes it. Being 'not my action' means that there is an "I" who does not act. It is ego to have an "I" who does not act.

Many people say, "I never did it." In spite of doing something, they say, "I have never done it." It is not that *I* have never done it. There is no "I" who acts, but there is an action. If somebody gets angry, the action of getting angry exists as a manifestation. However, there is no subject that got angry. There is no independent self that carried out an action.

Non-Possession

When thinking about non-possession, the first thing that comes to mind is the Venerable Beop-jeong, who deserves respect. From reading his books, he seems pure and beautiful in the way he tries so hard as a Buddhist monk. But from the perspective of truth, even though he is talking about non-possession, it is regrettable that he does not know real non-possession. He is actually talking about non-attachment and honest poverty. It means only "let us live with non-attachment and honest poverty" in both mind and material goods: a suit of clothes at least, one pair of shoes, one table with a kerosene lamp, as little food as possible. Then what is real non-possession? That is also "possession with no-self." It is a state that there is no "I" who possesses. Is there any possibility that someone does not possess anything in any way despite being living thing?

Was the Venerable Beop-jeong living naked? Did he just live in a field? Non-possession is different from honest poverty. Literally, if there is nothing to possess, he could not live.

The true meaning of non-possession is possession with no-self. It is, therefore, nonsense if it does not contain the word no-self. There is no "I" that possesses. Though I might live in a palace, it is not mine. Although there is a house, there is no "I" that possesses it. Even though I wear clothes, there is no subjective self that wears them. Therefore we cannot possess anything. How little do you have to have in order to live a poor but honest life?

For example, someone in a suit of clothes lives in a room of one square meter in order to live a poor but honest life. Compare this person to another wearing just short pants living in a half-meter square room—he is still not living with non-possession. It is just relative. It is, therefore, honest poverty with non-attachment, not true non-possession that Buddhism says is non-possession. True non-possession is possible only when there is no-self that possesses, even if there is possession.

Likewise its meaning becomes completely different. Is there any obstacle to the enlightened one? What are they afraid of and what can't they do? I have a car. Then how can I be said to have non-possession? However, even though there is a car, there is no "I" who possesses it. This word seems to be easy to understand, but in fact it is very hard. There is a very subtle nuance in that word. Obviously there is a car, but there is no "I" who owns it. When I do something, there is an action, but not an "I" who causes the action. That is no-self. Therefore we can understand correctly the meaning of such concepts having the word "nothing" only when we add the word "no-self" to them.

When Joju, a zen master, talked about nothing as *hua-tou*, the meaning of the word was not whether there is anything or not, but that there was no dualistic discrimination of being or not being. It is, therefore, called "the Absolute nothing," disconnected from dualistic discrimination. From such a perspective, we have to say the word "nothing."

To the question, "Does a dog have Buddha's nature?", though the zen master replied, "Nothing," you should not understand it as, "There is none of Buddha's nature in a dog." It means that there is no dualistic discrimination, whether there is or not Buddha's nature in a dog. He is saying, "You, idiot, do not make differentiations between this and that for the word 'nothing.'" This nothing is the Absolute nothing; the Absolute cut off from dualistic discrimination.

Non-Responsibility

Non-responsibility also is a word used wrongly by people now. It literally means being under no liability. Usually when we say, "That person is irresponsible," it means "That person holds no liability." But the word really means "That person is not responsible." Nonetheless, if saying, "You should live a responsible life; why are you so irresponsible?", it is an absurd expression,

because all events and connections that are projected and woven by the body-mind in the manifested world extend to thoughts and actions by the dependent origination principle. An individual entity has non-responsibility. However, there is no "I" as an individual entity having subjectivity. Of course, there exists an individual entity, but the entity does not have its own subjectivity. That means no "I," no self in that individual entity. So there is originally no subjective self taking responsibility. So there is non-responsibility. If you did something but are not responsible for it, then it is irresponsibility. Non-responsibility is because there is no "I" to be responsible. Why is there non-responsibility? Because it is not I that has done anything. Why did I not do it? Because I cannot be responsible for it due to being a no-subject. There is no person who shall be responsible because there is no doer. Because all has been done by the scenario itself.

The actor who committed murder in the play has done so according to the script, and a phenomenal action occurred. However, because it is a play, though the scene of the killing occurred, there is no real person who committed murder. And though there is the phenomenon of playing at being murdered, there is no dead person in reality. It is a hypothetic scenario. Can an illusionary entity be born and die? There is only the phenomenon that looks like it has been born and died. All living things in the universe are as such. That is because of illusions.

The true I, as reality, does not appear and disappear as an illusionary entity. Therefore reality does not become born and die; it is existence itself, life itself as it is, and so can never be hurt. It is only the phenomenon as an illusionary entity that is dead and disappears. From this perspective, when you see a play and say to the actor who played the murderer, "You are responsible for committing a sin and will be reborn as an animal due to the karma," this would be a funny story.

That is the dualistic discrimination of humanity. It is the discriminating mind that humanity is noble and animals are trivial. However all beings are the manifestations of true nature itself; human, animals, plants, stones. Though all beings are perfect, the reason why they are all different shapes is because their combinations of earth, water, fire, and air are different. Because of the perspective of dualistic discrimination, humanity just looks to be set above the rest while the others look trivial. It is like a liver seems important while an anus seems insignificant in the body; Buddha is holy and a prostitute is dirty. This is a discriminating mind. Buddha is just an illusion and a prostitute is also an illusion. They are just roles in the play. The roles are being played in the phenomenal world and shall be ended when the characters disappear.

Then is true nature good or bad? There is no such thing in true nature. Where then are good and evil? They are just relative concepts manifesting from relative beings into the relative universe. The true "I" cannot be affected by such good and evil as discrimination of the manifested world because of its true nature. So are you able to live without the effects of them? If you are not confident in doing so, your consciousness should be overturned. The consciousness of identifying one's self with this or that has to be completely changed. Or it will be no use even though you always recite the mantras, "I am true nature" or, "The body-mind is not mine." It is like children who try to memorize Chinese characters without knowing their meanings.

You have to overturn that consciousness with all your energy. I am true nature that cannot be affected by anything. I am a character in a play that has mistakenly identified myself with a body-mind complex. Why should the character be responsible for his role in the play? Though he committed robbery and murder in the play, he does not regret them, feel guilt or suffering. But there are some characters who think of themselves as really doing so in spite of merely playing their roles. It is very foolish. You need to overturn your consciousness completely. If you can stay in true nature, that is a great freedom. There is no obstruction for you. All things happen naturally. Because of no-self, all phenomena appear by themselves. With dependent origination the whole is one. However, in the state of individual consciousness, a person comes to identify themself with the thoughts and actions arising in themselves. That is ego.

In my mind a desire has arisen. Then it is ego that mistakenly thinks that I have caused that desire. An ego is not the attachment, but thinking of myself as having the attachment; ego is not dualistic discrimination but doing the dualistic discrimination. But nowadays religious groups still say, "Get rid of your greed." Who will throw away greed? Saying that must mean I am greedy, therefore they are saying to me to throw it away. There is, however, no "I" that clings to being greedy. Being greedy itself is arising only because of dependent origination and the role written by the scenario. I am greedy only in the play, but not in truth. Though a shadow is greedy, is it not a shadow? Although a shadow clings to something, is it also not still a shadow? It is, however, very simple when viewing all things as a kind of play.

But when thinking of myself as really doing something, suffering will follow. Because I have to be responsible for all. How can I not take responsibility for what I did? So I have to be responsible for all things because I mistakenly consider them as "I did" even though I did nothing, due to no-self. These are the worldly desires and sufferings of sentient beings. It is suffering for me to take responsibility for what I cannot be responsible for. Therefore, suffering does not exist in reality but only in the mind.

The minute one awakens from that illusion, all suffering will disappear. You do not need to remove something or do something hard to be free from suffering. The moment you realize, "Ah! this is illusion," all suffering will disappear.

Hega, disciple of the zen master Dharma, told Dharma, "Master, my mind is suffering so much."

Dharma answered, "Let me see your suffering mind, then I will get rid of the suffering." The moment he heard the answer, Hega's suffering disappeared. It is, therefore, enlightenment to be awakened from that illusion in the mind. It is not to arrive at somewhere, not to cultivate something hard, and not to sit cross-legged without sleeping. It is not necessary to do these. Why does Buddha try to be another Buddha even though he originally is Buddha? You only have to know that you yourself originally are Buddha.

Why is it that people cannot accept such an easy thing? It is because of the old established habit of mistakenly thinking of themselves as independent individuals. Because identifying one's self with this body-mind since being born has remained too strong, the ego, imaginary but originally not existing, can appear anytime. The word "I" always follows whenever saying anything, thinking, or acting. When removing that word "I," thinking, saying, and acting happen by themselves. Therefore we have to throw away that word. It does not exist fundamentally. It is only the Absolute, true nature that can be said to be "I."

Humanity has never been as no-true-nature even for a split second; has never existed as an ego even for a moment.

The Path of the Seeker

What is Enlightenment?

How will you be enlightened?

Just as it was getting dark, someone was walking along a mountain path. Then he saw something blocking the path that looked like a snake. He was too surprised and fearful to continue, but then someone came from the opposite direction. "Oh, how could you step across a snake on the road?" he asked. "Ah, that is not a snake but a straw rope," answered the other. Therefore the man went closer to see and realized it was really a straw rope.

Let's think about it. Was there really a snake? No. But the moment he misunderstood it as a snake, there was a snake in his mind. That is ego, individual consciousness. It exists only in misidentification. The snake originally did not exist but came about by misunderstanding and made him fearful. Likewise, the ego that does not truly exist makes humans suffer.

What is the only way to be awakened from the illusion that it is a snake? There is nothing to do but go and see. Of course, he can believe what the other person said, but it is not a 100% solution. The best and only way is to go and see yourself. It is as if the enlightened master says, "That is not a snake but a straw rope," and although I believe him I go see it myself. That is the most correct practice for seekers. The method of going and seeing like this is Vipassana meditation. The most important thing here is that Vipassana is not for cultivating the body-mind but just observing.

Therefore such general words like "cultivating" or "practicing" are not adequate. The most correct meaning of Vipassana is "awareness." Awareness, however, is possible only when the consciousness is awake. So the enlightened ones say, "Always be awake." Why should we always be awake? To see things as they are. However, a seeker who did not sleep and meditated for an overly long time due to the teacher's saying, "Always be awake," could even die from that. That would be foolish. Let us think about the situation of suffering; is there suffering while being awake? How about in deep sleep? There is suffering when we are already awake. Defilements and illusions also arise when waking. Even if someone has a big problem, they will be peaceful during sleep. Problems arise when waking. Therefore, to be always awake means not to mistakenly identify oneself with body-mind, but to be always in true nature, true "I." Vipassana is not just sitting and walking meditation.

Consciousness is to see the body-mind, all events and manifestations arising outside as they are, in the perspective of true nature. To see from true nature's perspective means to see in a pure state; to see things as they are without the thought or feeling of, "I did this," and to be aware of consciousness in true nature. When one loses awareness for a split-second, there arises again an illusion, because the consciousness identifies with the body-mind. If one maintains pure consciousness and sees the body-mind as it is, there will come a time one strongly feels that this body-mind is not "me." Then the identification of self with the body-mind will collapse in a moment, and the ego, the illusion of *I*—essentially not existing, only existing in a deluded mind—will be broken as if a rope you were holding snapped. You have to maintain awareness until enlightened.

What is the key point of Vipassana? It is to see birth-death; grasping the appearing-disappearing of all things. It is to see that all lives, material things, and manifestations arising in this phenomenal universe must die, as if noticing the rising and falling of the breath. If you recognize this birth-death correctly, you can be enlightened. What is the reason that one clings to *I*? It is because one does not deeply realize the impermanence of this body-mind—that it is born and then must die—understanding it only as knowledge or a word. The enlightened know in their heads that the whole is one, "I" is true nature and this body is just an illusion that will come and go. Nonetheless, you may still struggle to escape mistakenly identifying yourself as an individual entity.

If you are trapped in the limits of ego, even a long sitting meditation without sleep for 40 to 50 years will be no use. In Myanmar, there are many fortunate people who have been practicing Vipassana for over ten years. Monks of 70 or 80 years old are doing walking meditation with a cane or staff, even though they cannot walk very well. It is like the Korean monks who cling to their *hua-tou (kong-an)* until their last breath. It looks horrible. What is the problem? No matter how long one practices within the limits of ego, it is no use. Then how can we know the truth? We should be able to see the universe as a whole. Then you will know that all things in the phenomenal universe are reasonably functioning in good order.

Then what do we realize? It doesn't matter if we practice Vipassana or *hua-tou* zen for decades. The important thing is what we have to realize. When you know the right way to the summit of the mountain, you can reach it; you cannot get there without knowing the right way, no matter how much you wander here and there. We need to take the right path. Then what should we realize? No-self. There is no more simple way than no-self, a condensed version of Buddha's teaching. However, after enlightenment I was very surprised that people interpreted such a simple term as being very complicated.

What is no-self? It means that there is no "I." What is I? It means I as an individual existence. The only thing that should be called I is the Absolute, true nature. That is true "I." There is no dualistic discrimination, you and me, in it. There is no I as an independent entity existing separately; this one sentence is the conclusion of all enlightenment. I finished my path of seeking by realizing this one sentence. Anybody can do it if realizing this one point.

If you read the books written by great Buddhist monks, no-self is interpreted as "removing self by cultivating." It is very disappointing. No-self does not mean removing one's self by cultivating, but by originally being not a self. How can you remove "I" (self) if it originally does not exist? Couldn't you remove it only if it exists? It is ridiculous. If there is I, ego, all those who have practiced sitting meditation for a long time could have removed it. Such people devoting themselves to practicing meditation could do anything. However, it is impossible: they are trying to remove what does not exist.

After enlightenment I do not know how much I laughed. I had wandered around to remove myself, not even existing for 25 years. Was there anything to do other than laugh when I realized no-self? It is impossible for me to describe all my feelings at that moment. Some may ask, "Why is that? Then everything, including Vipassana, is no use, because there is originally nothing?" This, however, is not the case. Your heart must be completely relieved. The moment you are enlightened, you might feel strongly refreshed in your heart. It seems that a rope holding you has snapped and disappeared. The reason that I explain this in detail is so that you can practice correctly, at least in knowledge. When you understand the right concepts and remain awake through Vipassana, someday your heart shall meet no-self. That is the day when you will become enlightened. The less-evolved devotee will use this knowledge upon hearing it and say they are enlightened, but such folk will not even be able to approach enlightenment.

Enlightenment is possible only when exploring with 100% purity, 100% eagerness, and 100% patience.

These three elements are a necessity for the true seeker. Let's look at them in more detail.

Three elements for the true seeker

First is purity: being pure-hearted. It means that for the mind to accept the truth it has to be purified beforehand. If even a little remains of one's petty spiritual experiences, religious doctrines, or academic achievements, there is no space for the pure truth to enter. Therefore, all enlightened ones have urged as a priority, "Be like a child." The seeker must not judge the truth by his own partial knowledge and fixed ideas.

Let us take an enlightened master of the late 20th century, Nisargadatta Maharaj. He dropped out of primary school and worked at someone else's home as a servant. To support his family he made leaf tobacco to sell. One day, at his friend's suggestion, he went to meet a guru. The guru said, "You are the Absolute and all things came from it. You are the true nature, not an impermanent being to be born and die. You are an everlasting being, the Absolute." Maharaj accepted his master's words 100 percent. He believed in his master's saying without any judgment even though he did not know whether it was true or not. His master died a few months after their meeting. However, Maharaj had explored his master's words for himself for three years and became enlightened. How pure he was! If you really wish to be enlightened, you have to be like Maharaj. You should open your heart without judging in your head. Then the truth will get through your heart.

Second is eagerness: being desperate. The true seeker must keep in their mind an eagerness for the truth. They have to explore it with all their heart. It must not be approached with a mindset of, "OK, I will give it a try," after doing all the other things they wanted to do. You should not think the truth is going to be that easy. Only after very painstaking practice and enormous effort will the truth be realized. It does not matter where your body is. Because each has their own role. Eagerness and purity for the truth must continue to occupy the seeker's mind. I had also lived like this for 25 years. Though I wandered in wrong directions, not meeting the truth, I was always full of eagerness for it in my heart. When doing it this way, the truth shall be realized. It will not happen by itself in spite of carrying out any specific scenario.

Third is patience: continuing to the end, until becoming enlightened. This patience encompasses the meaning of not being in a hurry. Buddhism says, "Go alone, like a rhino's horn." Have you ever seen a cow hurry? They walk tirelessly with dignified step. Therefore, the journey of the seeker is not so easy. You should not hurry: go forward without haste. But this does not mean you can explore idly doing anything you want. It means that you do your best but do so naively and honestly, without haste. So it is very difficult. When I said I was enlightened in just one month after practicing meditation in Myanmar, some may wonder why they cannot be enlightened when I reached it so early. No, it took me 25 years. I had been walking the path seeking the truth for 25 years. It was like picking a ripe fruit when I was enlightened within a month of Vipassana meditation in Myanmar, only picking the fruit through the last meditation of awareness. But before it all was the process of preparation. This was not enlightenment through just one month of practice, but putting a dot on my path by practicing

Vipassana meditation for a month. So do not hurry. Though I wandered around through many religious groups, I did not find the truth. I made the decision that if I could not meet the true master, "I will do it all by myself, even in the mountains, and if I die without enlightenment, I will do it again after rebirth." As such, you have to do it naively and honestly.

Each person has to do their best in their own situation. Vipassana is not just sitting with crossed legs, but also witnessing the movement of body-mind in the consciousness, always based on the true nature in any activity, with anybody, and in any situation. See it as it is without thinking of it as "myself doing it." It does not need any other time and effort, but it needs an eagerness for the truth. If you explore the truth deeply and with eagerness day by day, month by month, you will be realized automatically. Enlightenment will arise by itself when doing it this way.

Your worldly activity is an assigned role. It is no use blaming your role. You can only act with an eager mind in each given situation. The seeker must not blame the situation, because all things can be used for your spiritual practice. The true seeker must accept everything confronted as an opportunity to learn. Though I spent my all youth in religions, I never regretted it: "I have learned so much there but will never be deceived again." Because I came to know that was not truth, I accepted it simply as my learning. By doing this, the seeker will grow and then the fruit of the truth can ripen.

However you meet the truth now, what a wonder it is! I am now throwing the truth to you as it is. If I could not understand something when reading books, I felt a pressure on my chest; having no choice but to read it repeatedly because there was no one to ask. But you have a master who can answer your questions and guide you onto the right path. There are so many people who have wandered around in confusion. Though you met the best conditions to find the path, if you cannot be enlightened, you are incorrigible.

You always check these three required conditions: purity, eagerness, patience.

Do you surrender 100 percent to the truth given by your master?

Are you in a state of eagerness for the truth?

Are you doing your best here and now?

Is your consciousness always awake, to see reality as it is?

Vipassana Meditation (Insight Meditation)

There are largely two categories among the many kinds of meditations in the world: Samatha (concentration) and Vipassana (insight). In order to be enlightened, there must be a harmonious practice between these two types of meditations. It is, however, regrettable that most practice nowadays is limited to Samatha (concentration). One may experience a deep concentration through Samatha practice but cannot realize no-self, true nature, because one will lose the insight to realize true nature due to the deep concentration. The reason why Buddha said, "Practice both *samadhi* and *sati* [insight]," is because one can be enlightened only when practicing both Samatha and Vipassana.

In Samatha practice, there is prayer, Buddhist chanting, yoga, hypogastric breathing (*danjeon*), mind control, and *hua-tou* zen. One can be enlightened, of course, by such practices, or without any specific practice. It is, however, very difficult to realize no-self through this Samatha even with lifelong practice, though there can be secondary effects, such as the power to see past or future lives, a temporarily peaceful mind, and health.

Then what is Vipassana, insight meditation, which Buddha himself practiced and taught his disciples? This practice is the one at the highest level that harmonized Samatha and Vipassana at the same time; practicing simultaneously both *samadhi* (concentration) and *sati* (mindfulness). The Buddha practiced Samatha in the beginning through six years of asceticism in the woods, but came to know that he could not attain enlightenment by doing so. He, therefore, changed it into Vipassana under a bodhi tree and then realized the true nature to set up the perfect truth of no-self, dependent origination, and the middle way. He taught Vipassana to his disciples as insight meditation. It is, however, regrettable that it has come to be a kind of technique remaining as a shell some 2500 years later. Though it is a great meditation practice, if one forgets the fundamental teaching and just falls into the technique, then one cannot attain enlightenment. Because even Buddha, a master, or Vipassana are kinds of provisional practices to attain enlightenment—if one attaches or clings to even a little thing, true nature cannot be revealed. When one can observe it as it is without attachment, then enlightenment will be revealed by itself.

Observing the fourfold stages of mindfulness means to see

all phenomena that appear and vanish in the body, sensation, mind, and Dharma (that is, things in general), as they are; just be mindful of them without attachment, overlooking, being affected, or discriminating.

Vipassana meditation consists of three sections: sitting practice, walking practice, and daily life practice. When performing sitting meditation, there are a few possible postures like cross-legged, half cross-legged, etc; you can choose one as you want. Close your eyes gently, keep your back straight, and fold your hands or lay them on your thighs.

Sitting meditation is basically to observe the breathing. You should not try to change the manner of natural breathing, just keep in mind the rise and fall of the abdomen. While you are mindful of "rising" on breathing in and "falling" on breathing out, if the mind begins to think of something else then it should be noted, calling it "thinking, thinking," and then return to the usual practice of noticing rising and falling as soon as the movements become clear again. When it is found again that the mind has noticed some feeling, like pain or itching, it should be noted as "painful, painful," or "itching, itching."

You should not hurry to respond to the feelings arising in the mind-body. For observing the truth that everything arising must also vanish, you should just observe any event arising as it is. You should not cling to or remove thinking or feeling pain, but just note and observe. Then the feelings will disappear by themselves. Because you do not note the impermanence of body-mind as arising and vanishing by itself, you mistakenly identify "yourself" with the existence that causes such feelings.

But if you deeply note and observe, you will know that there is no "I" as an independent entity but only the functioning of consciousness in the body-mind that continuously arises and vanishes. If you sit for a long time and cannot tolerate the leg pain, you should note it fully to change the posture, naming it as "posture change, posture change." And then the usual excercise of noticing the rising and falling of the abdomen should be reverted to. Though in the beginning you may not note many things, if you keep practicing, you will note and observe minutely all feelings arising.

Walking meditation is divided into three stages. The first stage is that you should note each step as "left step, right step" while walking. When you feel that you want to stop, you should make a note of "wanting to stop," and note it as "stop" if you stop the walk. Then slowly scan and observe the body from head to feet. When wanting to turn, note it as "wanting to turn" and note as "turning, turning" while actually turning. At the second stage, a note should be made on two sections, in each step as "lifting, dropping." For the third stage, each step should be noted as three divided sections of "lifting, moving forward, dropping." If you see something while walking, you stop and note "seeing, seeing;" likewise "hearing, hearing" if hearing something, "thinking, thinking" if thinking. Also note conditions such as "windy, windy" when noticing the wind, then revert to the usual noting movement of the feet.

Vipassana can be practiced in daily life. In the morning you can start as you wake up from sleep. Note "waking up" and then continue to note, like "opening eyes, sitting up, folding bedding, feeling thirsty, seeing refrigerator, opening refrigerator door, holding water bottle, shutting the door, pouring water, drinking water, putting down glass," etc. All daily life should be noted: washing face, eating food, putting on clothes, using the bathroom, etc., except sleeping time. Among the four stages of mindfulness, you note just one that may be most strongly cognized and then you should observe another one soon.

Of course, you might miss many things in the beginning, but later you will note minutely the movements through continuous practice and gain the wisdom to realize no-self, dependent origination and the middle way as your insight deepens.

Living the discipline of the seeker

First, act as if not seeing, not hearing, and not having a mouth even though you do see, hear, and have a mouth.

Second, move slowly and cautiously.

Third, do not have curiosity or interfere in others' concerns.

The Moment of Enlightenment

I would like to talk about my path of practice as a seeker. I especially want to share my practice diary, which has recorded insights and notions attained through Vipassana meditation. Those pieces of knowledge and experience will surely be helpful to you in realizing no-self. But there are not many stories because it took just one month for me to attain enlightenment in Myanmar. However, I will try to explain in detail for your better understanding. As this experience is a real story, you should take my words to heart and make them your guide to your search for truth.

Since I became a Christian at 15 years old, I spent my youth absorbed in eastern-western religion and philosophy. However, I finished my religious life of 20 years after recognizing that there is no religion that tells the truth. I threw myself into the world to make money for five years, but it made me taste the bitterness of life. When I was suffering and getting tired at 40 years old, a feeling of doubt occurred to me inside. "This is not my way. What am I doing as a seeker?" I stopped all I had been doing and restarted my path to seek truth.

I devoted myself to spiritual practice again and almost got rid of the attachment to worldly life. Nevertheless the subtle ego remained to torture me, and I thought only complete enlightenment could ultimately solve suffering. After about one-and-a-half years of practicing again, I came to discover the books of Maharshi and Maharaj. When I read them books I was very surprised. "Oh, my, how come I never found such books until now?" However, this was lucky for me—if I had read them a long time ago, I would not have understood them. Through looking back on my seeking journey, what a miraculous scenario it was; when absolutely necessary, there occurred a meeting of such incidents and relationships. Sometimes I fell into a ditch, or received gifts, and then ultimately came to find the books of the enlightened.

Though I had practiced Samatha for a long time, a delicate ego remained. And so, in spite of getting rid of attachment, something subtle still drove me distracted. At the time when I was distressed by this, I came to find all the books of Maharshi and Maharaj, and Vipassana within a month. Although the truth shown by Maharshi and Maharaj was the most valuable treasure, it was not easy to practice the mind observation and the self-exploration that they proposed. In the meantime I read the book of Vipassana, which touched my heart. "Yes! There must be some solution for Buddha's enlightenment." Until then I did not know how Buddha had attained enlightenment. Most Buddhists did not know this either. If you ask Buddhists about it, there are many who believe Buddha practiced *hua-tou* zen. However, in reality, Buddha practiced Vipassana meditation. At that time I had already practiced Samatha for a long time and so I had come to accept it as it was. This feeling came to me: "Yes, truth is to see as it is, not something that can be worked towards and attained."

"This is it, at last I have found it!" I shouted. I flew to Myanmar, saying, "I will go and practice the Vipassana that Buddha himself did and became enlightened." I thought it would take maybe about a year at that time. Though I thought my practice had almost become ripe and there was no more attachment, that subtle ego had been on my mind until then. And although I understood no-permanence, I really could not do no-self. Because when realizing no-self, ego would disappear. Therefore I went to Myanmar in order to solve this problem.

That is how I went to the Mahashi meditation center in Myanmar and started practicing Vipassana.

Nov. 4, 1998
Arriving at Mahashi Meditation Center
The first day there was an orientation for newcomers and meditation started the next day. While attending school before I did not like to write, using just one notebook for a year. However, for some reason I wanted to write a diary during my stay there, so I did. I did not write every day but only when I had strong feelings. It is lucky that I can show my diary now.

Nov. 5, 1998

Feeling pins and needles in my legs, sore joints, and sore back due to sudden long practice (sleeping for just four hours a day).

The first day I wrote just that one sentence. I had never slept so few hours. Before going to Myanmar, I usually slept for six to eight hours a day. However, here as much as four hours' sleeping was unusual for me. I spent all the first day fighting pain in my body. So when I saw other newcomers I thought they would have a hard time, too. Anyway, the first day was quite hard on me, because I had not been practicing much sitting meditation, and practicing throughout the day was even harder for me. Besides, I usually used a bed and sofa at home and so was not used to sitting on the floor. It was usually 30 to 40 degrees in Myanmar. If you sat for one hour, the sitting cushion would get wet with perspiration. Moreover, my body ached and I could not communicate for one week, being unable to speak either English or the language of Myanmar. After three or four days I regretted having come; if I had stayed home I would not be having such a hard time. After all, I spent the first days struggling with pain.

Nov. 6, 1998

Sleepy when sitting meditation. Continuous cramp in the left little finger.

When I was working in business, I played golf, which usually requires strength in the left hand. I had not had the habit of much physical exercise, but suddenly using my left hand much more caused a bit of problem in that hand. While practicing meditation, there usually occurs some phenomenon at the beginning from a weak part of the body when the energy circulates within the body. From the following day an abnormal phenomenon began to occur; I kept feeling cramps and shaking in my left finger.

Pricking on the back of neck and face. And shoulder discomfort.
As if I had been beaten hard, I ached all over, even walking slowly, feeling more pain than when I had done physical labor in the past.

When observing breathing with back straight, I felt feverish and as if floating in the air.
Such a feeling came to me very fast, while I ached all over with abnormal sensations and the energy was circling all over my body.

Being conscious of only above the neck but not of the other parts of the body and feeling only pain in the legs. After observing breathing for a while, shifted to the pain in the legs to note the pain moving fast from ankle to pelvic bones many times.
Though a strong pain was arising, I could not feel anything in my body because of practicing
Samadha. Without feeling the body, there was only the con-

sciousness of feeling pain in such a state. By just the second day, such phenomena began to occur very fast. When hearing my interview with Ven. Sayadaw, the practice leader, other people who had been practicing for six months were surprised, because I had observed and noted within just a week what they usually had in one or two months. I was making more rapid progress than others.

Nov. 7, 1998

Noting that I was frequently changing my posture due to feeling more pain during sitting meditation. Practicing walking meditation in three stages for twenty minutes each. While practicing sitting meditation, I observed breathing with my hands on my abdomen due to not noting it well. Trying to breathe artificially.

There occurred many problems at first because I became mindful of many things. Due to the aching in my legs, I kept changing my sitting position. Would I be able to reach the *samadhi* in this situation? When I asked a question about it during an interview with Ven. Sayadaw he said, "Do not change frequently, only once an hour." I replied, "Yes, I will try," and did so, despite the pain. If you make up your mind as such: "I will do so," then you can do it. Of course, it is not your own volition but you can do it because consciousness notes it.

Nov. 10, 1998

Pain in the legs somewhat relieved. Starting a sitting meditation and doing yoga every time after finishing.

I thought it was better to do sitting meditation while applying pressure to my painful leg, rather than discontinuing. Therefore I did yoga before and after, and the leg pain got much better from relaxing the muscles. Daily schedule: get up at 3 o'clock in the morning, first meditation at 4 o'clock for one hour, then soup for breakfast, and meditation again from 6 to 9 o'clock; sitting, walking, sitting for one hour each, take a shower and have a second meal, and start meditation again from 11 AM to 5 PM; walking, sitting, walking and sitting for one hour each, and then take a shower at 5 o'clock in the afternoon, start meditation from 6 to 11 o'clock in the evening and then sleep: in total there were 13 hours of meditation per day. There were only two meals; no food after noon. So from the outset I had only two meals a day. I got so sweaty, and felt severe stomach ache around four in the afternoon. But in three days I got used to this way of living and in ten days I felt comfortable enough to practice well; I realized all my problems came from habit. The shooting pain in the face and finger cramps disappeared. And the shoulder discomfort was also cured due to the good flow of body energy.

Then there was the question of how I would be able to observe while talking, reading, and sleeping, for when I read a book I tend to fall into whatever I am reading. For me, until that point the Buddhist exhortation had constantly been in my mind—"*o-me-il-yeo*" (always be aware whether awake or asleep). I had been really curious about this because I had thought of having to always observe mindfully, whether waking or sleeping, and heard that I could be enlightened only when becoming a state of *o-me-il-yeo*. I thought that I had to observe even when sleeping in order to be enlightened. When I raised this point to Sayadaw (our practice leader), he said, "Sleep only while sleeping" which helped me a lot. I fully accepted his answer. How can you observe while sleeping without even being conscious? If I could pick out the most helpful advice I received from Sayadaw during my stay in Myanmar, it would be this: "Sleep only while sleeping." I also noticed several changes or signs during sitting meditation; a strongly beating pulse and breathing like waves continuously rising and falling on the surface of the sea.

When performing sitting and walking meditation, there arose many thoughts into which I fell and came to notice later, coming back to call them, "thinking, thinking."
At first, everybody experiences falling into thoughts and only notices them later, thinking, "What was I doing?" It is important, however, to notice and come back again, even if it is later. By continuing to come back and notice, you will not be lost in thoughts any more. At first anybody will end up lost in thoughts.

There arose again a pain, like needling on my face, while doing sitting meditation.
I thought the abnormal phenomenon had disappeared but it

came back. It came not just once but continuously. Sometimes I had a feeling of gladness while falling into *samadhi*. It is an important fact that most people psychologically want to maintain the state of *samadhi* once it has come. But you should not. You should note the state of feeling of gladness now and accept that the appearance must disappear. If you do not accept the fact, you will come to cling to it in the future. If you can note and observe the appearing-disappearing of such feelings of gladness during practice, you will not cling so much to the same feelings in life. Because practice and life are not different, it is not possible that you will do well during practice yet not do well in life.

When thinking of others and myself during sitting meditation, I felt sad.

Without any reason I felt sad. There arose many sad thoughts, like floating clouds. It is usual that this sort of thing happens to seekers during their practice.

So many kinds of delusions arising because of moving to a different place.

The yearly national meeting of all Mahasi meditation centers was going to start there on November 30. During that time, many people from more than a hundred branches would attend, so it would be too noisy to practice. Most people decided they would move to another meditation center for the duration. I felt my concentration on practice seeming to scatter because I was thinking about the change of lodging.

Nov. 11, 1998

Observing my breathing is very irregular.

During practice I began to note that my breathing was very irregular; long breaths or short, strong or weak, delicate, feeling abdominal swelling, etc.

While practicing walking meditation, I came to note the movement of every step as divided into three stages; lifting, moving forward, and dropping the foot.

When practicing walking meditation, I moved each step as three stages; lift, forward, and drop. At first I just noted each stage, but then came to also notice the movement of each stage according to my call. I noted the reason why each step was divided into two or three stages named this way. When we move one step, actually it is not a single movement but many connected sections within it.

If we make a movie with a camera and develop the film, we note that one movement is made of many individual frames. We can see the same thing if we note and observe minutely through practicing Vipassana. Even in a movement there are so many things arising and vanishing. When turning back in a walking meditation and calling it, "turning, turning," I noted that this movement was also made of connections of many births and deaths. If you can note and observe this in either sitting or walking meditation, you will be able to note the same in any other meditation. That will be a miracle. Why? Because consciousness along the same level is all connected.

While doing a sitting meditation, I was captured by many

delusions that occurred without my being mindful.

During the one hour of sitting meditation I found I could observe and note well for twenty minutes but for forty minutes I could not; I was captured by delusions. Thinking back, it seemed like a mess; sometimes I was sleepy or lost in thought, or changing my posture due to feeling pain. Sometimes even for ten solid minutes I was unable to observe and note. It was torturous for me. Because of the fear of losing face I would sit against my will without saying anything. However the seeker has to experience such processes in order to help become intense.

Appearing and Disappearing are noted as being like the pendulum in a clock swinging back and forth.

I felt that appearing-disappearing seemed like a pendulum swinging back and forth on a clock. Maybe it seemed like that because I felt bored; continuing with "rising, falling" made me feel like this. Because I observed breathing well, then I thought, "OK, let's keep going like the pendulum in a clock." This came because there had been something accepted within me during practice.

Nov. 12, 1998

Interview with Sayadaw

Because I had been observing my breathing well, I noted a gap between rising and falling. When interviewing with Sayadaw, I mentioned this and he taught me that I should observe the sitting period between breaths and if observing well, then go into detail like this, "rising, sitting, falling, sitting." It would be less boring, he said, so I tried it and was able to block distracting thoughts this way. And he gave another piece of advice: when breathing is becoming longer, it is better to observe in many divided steps, like "rising, rising, rising…"

While observing like this I noted that breathing in or out is linked to so many births-deaths. This cannot be explained in words but can only be directly observed. You have to note that the birth-death is repeated countless times in each moment. Vipassana means to see the birth-death occurring in all phenomena. The birth-death is not just a singular event—we need to see many births-deaths even in a birth, as well as in a death. And then you will note that everything is in birth-death. When you understand birth-death to this depth, you will realize impermanence itself.

Nov. 13, 1998
While doing a walking meditation, the feelings of cold, softness, hardness, heat, etc., are only the phenomena felt on objects upon contact, not the inherent nature of the body-mind.
Mindfulness is like this. I was able to note that such feelings on my feet upon contacting objects while walking are just phenomena, not inherent nature. Such noticing will be manifested from various angles on the way to enlightenment. It is important to feel, note, accept, and understand as such, gradually.

In breathing the falling begins at the end of the rising.
In fact, this is natural. Why did I note such a natural phenomenon at that time? It means I had not actually realized it until then. Mindfulness has to be experienced and realized. Even such a simple event had to be noted. At that time I had formed a new habit; looking often at the clock due to the pain in my legs. While doing sitting meditation, I felt bored and so looked at the clock thinking, "Why is the time so long?" That night I thought, "How can I become enlightened when I can't even sit for one hour? I need to settle the matter." There was a three-hour practice from six to nine in the evening. So I thought of continuing a sitting meditation for three hours that time, even if my legs broke. Imagine how much leg pain I would feel sitting continuously for thirteen hours a day if I could not even get used to sitting just for one hour. I could not tolerate the leg pain any more, so it began as soon as I sat. Strange to say, when thinking of the pain, the legs know it in advance and feel the pain almost in anticipation. Even posing in the sitting meditation, the pain would begin. This means that the pain is closely connected to the mind. That was why I decided to practice the sitting meditation continuously for three hours.

My body swayed back and forth, left and right in a circle from 1:30 to 2:30 PM during a sitting meditation.
Samathi came even as I was feeling strong pain, because I kept at the meditation. In *samathi* I felt the body moving left-right in a circle due to the energy moving within it, but let it do so. When I noted the energy moving, it stopped moving. While re-

verting to the usual exercise of noting "rising, falling," the body again moved as such, and that continued to occur. I kept noting the rising and falling of my abdomen and the rising and vanishing of pain in the meditation, and then seemed to feel my body floating above the floor. I understood then the claims that people experience levitation during spiritual practice, but in fact it was an experience of consciousness. My body seemed to float in the air. There was no feeling, only the consciousness of floating. The breathing was ever-changing; gradually fast and then stopping for a while. That continuing no-breathing made me think, "This is a big problem and I will die if I don't breathe." But there was no feeling like suffocating. Then there occurred a sudden breath by itself.

Such happenings were not intended but came naturally. If only noting my breathing changed so much, I felt very peaceful. *Samathi* occurred by itself when just noting and observing, but not by any intention.

Nov. 14, 1998

There was a Dharma talk (a lecture on Buddha's teachings) at 4 o'clock in the afternoon. Usually Sayadaw, the elder of the center, would give the talk but he was absent at that time, so a young monk did it instead. He gave the speech in English but I could not understand English well. I was completely broken that day. Let us see my diary of the day below.

I attended the Dharma talk for the first time at Mahashi Med-

itation Center. A young Myanmar monk gave a lecture, about 80 minutes. It was terrible that I sat on my knees on the hard floor for 80 minutes—what was worse I could not understand the English. While it felt like my pelvis, knees and ankles were breaking, the lecture kept going, slowly, even after the finishing bell had already rung. I felt doubt within, "Why did I come here to practice looking so miserable, and bow three times to this unknown young monk." After coming back to my room, I thought deeply and recognized that it was a significant event of great change within. Though I did not note it at that time, it was good work. I had had to listen to the English speech as a mere sound, note the pain, and feel the sense of unity without I-am-ness in bowing three times. I thought I could deal better with the next Dharma talk.

There is a traditional Myanmar sitting posture like a woman sitting on her knees, hips to the side. While the monk gave the Dharma talk, everyone including the men were supposed to sit like this. I had never sat like that. People of the southern countries seem not to hurry, and he continued for an extra 20 minutes, even though the bell had already rung. I felt pain in my pelvis and joints due to sitting like that on the hard wooden floor. "How hateful he is!" I thought. I felt defeated as I came back to my room, because I could not say or understand anything in English.

At that time I felt so miserable, getting angry at the many complex situations, because of my conscious thinking of myself as the seeker. After returning to my room I came to observe this in my mind, and there arose the thought, "Did I come here in order to be treated well or to be recognized by someone? Can I not tolerate just 80 minutes, despite always saying that all things can be good for spiritual practice?" Seekers sometimes experience things like this. As long as the ego remains, such self-respect often arises. However, the event did initiate some progress in my practice of Vipassana.

I could concentrate better in sitting meditation and so continued sitting meditation for two hours with mindfulness. The leg pain was getting stronger and moving here and there around the body.

The pain did not occur in one place on the body but moved around. If noting it, then I could observe it in detail. I thought, "If the pain is felt, how can I tolerate it?" However, when I could concentrate well and fall into *samathi*, I was not troubled despite the great pain, only taking note of it.

But it was not moving. Because the pain occurred and disappeared rapidly and then another pain was soon felt, it was felt mistakenly, like it was moving about.

At first I thought the pain was moving around but then observed and noted that a pain would arise and vanish, and then another one was noted; many pains arose and vanished rapidly and consciousness followed them, but it was not one pain moving around. It meant that mindfulness was gaining strength and adding detail. It had been 11 days since I started the practice, during which I had been fighting pain and lack of sleep, but this seemed surely to be progress. There followed an observation that had seemed impossible before.

The pains appearing continuously like waves of the sea were not the same in feeling, strength, and manifestation. While the pains were getting strong, the observation came true in a state of no-breathing after just one breathing in and out.

Before, my breath kept going in a straight line, like a dead man's wavelength in an electrocardiogram, but now, after a breath in and out I was able to observe and note the pain in a state of no-breathing. Because I was achieving such close observation, the breathing came to stop by itself.

Breath, pain, and thought are vividly noted to be just a few among the many manifestations that appear and disappear by themselves in the body-mind according to dependent origination.

My observation and notice began to arrive at the truth. All such as breath, pain, and thoughts are just phenomena that appear and vanish by themselves in the body-mind, and their appearances came in various manifestations.

Nov. 16, 1998

While sitting in meditation for one hour and 40 minutes, rising-falling was becoming fast and later disappeared, without being named. Breathing stopped and observing continued, and I noted that breathing in arose and disappeared rapidly and so did breathing out. Mindfulness and notice were becoming more detailed.

Now there was no more regular practice in sitting and walking meditation; sitting meditation continued usually for one or two hours, forgetting about the time. The pain still arising could not no longer disturb *samathi*.

Nov. 17, 1998

When hearing crows cawing outside during sitting meditation, I noticed the sound arising and vanishing. Breathing also is on a continuum of appearing-disappearing within a moment. Therefore there is no past and future in life. Only now and here exists because all things occur in a split-second.

This was not realization, but what I began to see was that existence is the moment itself; it only seems to be a time consisting of many moments. Life itself is also not a continuum of time. However, we generally think of existence as a time-continuum consisting of past, present, and future.

A delusion is a phenomenon. Only be mindful and concentrate without clinging to it and trying to remove it.

This shows that wisdom arises in its own time while we observe and note. When we practice, we usually try to remove the delusions that arise. But now I can see that a delusion is only a phenomenon. And so we should not think of it as defilement. There is no difference between thought and delusion. There exists only thought. Because of dualistic discrimination that something is not a good thought, we name it a delusion, but there is no good thought and no bad one. If you say, "They are same as the phenomenal, but…" then it reveals that you mean dualistic discrimination.

We should say only in the view of truth. While observing, there is a big difference between one who thinks of things as delusions and one who considers them to be thoughts. If noting something as "thinking," we see it as a phenomenon, but if noting as "delusion," we see it as a bad thought. Is there defilement? The enlightened one sees it as a *bodhi* (wisdom); defilement therefore means wisdom. Buddha is not separated from sentient beings. Buddha is not different to sentient beings. If we say in the view of the Absolute or in the view of the relative, that means dualistic discrimination. The answer should be only one; the Absolute is the true self. Therefore we should speak only at the Absolute level.

If you are in the view of the Absolute, the relative becomes the truth because the relative is as it is. Only when seen at the Absolute level does the relative become the Absolute. However, if you are viewing the relative world without perceiving the Absolute, there is nothing to come from that other than dualistic discrimination. That is important. So your consciousness should stay in a view of the Absolute. If a thought arises within you to kill someone you try to remove it, noting, "delusion, delusion," because you mistakenly think of it as a bad thought. From where did the thought arise? You think it came from your mind, but is this body-mind you? If it is not you, why are you surprised? There is only one reason—identifying yourself with that thought. We should discard such mistaken ideas.

After arising, vanishing does not begin; appearing and disappearing are simultaneous.

From now on, because my mindfulness is growing strong, please pay careful attention.

Birth-death is working simultaneously during breathing in, as well as in breathing out.

While doing a walking meditation, there is simultaneously working an appearing-disappearing at the moment of lifting a foot. It is not that there is appearing when lifting a foot or disappearing when putting it down, but there is appearing and disappearing at the same time. When a bird begins singing, appearing and disappearing work simultaneously. Awareness should become like this; at the beginning it should be perceived gradually in consecutive order and then simultaneously.

While walking in the meditation hall, the feeling on the floor was warm, but it was cold and hard when walking out in the corridor. This is just a phenomenon appearing according to the feeling of touching the object.

This is very simple. They are felt as they are. Practicing Vipassana begins like this; observation is simple and clear like a child's. The stronger the observation, the more it becomes simple and clear. You can see as it is.

It is noted that the feeling is not controlled by the body but it should be accepted as it is when objects are contacted.

We should accept it as it is. It is a feeling of natural and dependent origination, arising in a meeting between a natural phenomenon and a physical one, that we dislike the cold or the heat felt from the objects. However, let us say that the mind refused it and then there arose annoyance. Is it right or wrong that such annoyance arose? Though such annoyance or cursing arose, those are just phenomena arising in the mind. Did I make them arise? Because I did not, I should not interfere in their arising.

However it is not easy to do this. As I said before, I was angry and annoyed due to the overrunning of the Dharma talk. At that time, had I noted it as "annoyed, annoyed," there would be no problem, but I did not do so and regretted having considered myself a so-called seeker. Who was annoyed? It was merely a phenomenon. Then why the regret? Because of mistakenly identifying yourself with the annoyance, you self-identify with the body-mind. Therefore, if you are not able to see true nature, you have no choice but to be this way.

Nov. 19, 1998

Arising feels light but falling away heavy.

When breathing in I felt very light and soft, but when breathing out, very heavy; mindfulness was getting strong and becoming instinctive. Walking meditation was the same; I felt light when lifting my foot, and heavy when putting it down.

When breathing and noting "rising, falling, rising, falling," at first I felt that breathing is like flowing water and later that

it stops many times. After continuing to observe, I perceived breathing very softly and clearly, like marbles rolling on a road.

It is not a common feeling that minute cells feel like they are sputtering. It is different each time depending on the given situation. When feeling sharply that the phenomenon is arising, the tiny differences are noted. It is part of the process of gaining *samathi; both* samathi *and awareness* are working together. Just accept situations as they are.

Nov. 20, 1998

After breakfast at six in the morning, it was so funny to look at myself practicing a sitting meditation. Trying to attain nirvana was really something to see. What is nirvana? Does it mean being free without any attachment? Now, human beings cannot even do nothing. If nirvana were something to attain, it seemed that doing it would be all the easier. By practicing hard we can attain samathi but cannot attain nirvana. Because we keep our life habits, acquired in the same way as we learned the alphabet and multiplication table, etc., we have to train ourselves even for letting go of all things. It is very hard to experience through the heart even though it is quick for the head to understand. Therefore the head and the words always precede the attainment. nirvana does not come up in the future. When you let go of all things and see everything here and now, all defilements disappear and emptiness—nirvana—comes up simultaneously.

From that moment, it looked miserable for me as I tried so hard to be enlightened. There arose a fickle mind, and habitual bragging about knowledge.

After thirty minutes of sitting meditation during the day, I had to stop because I felt heat in my body and could no longer stand it.

Sometimes during meditation there arises a fire in the body like a furnace, and sometimes cold is felt. Many other subtle kinds of phenomena come up, impossible to express. You have to see them as simple phenomena that appear during practice. If you think of them as magic and cling to them, you come to lose your way. Sometimes you can read the mind of the person next to you while you are developing *samathi*, and if you cling to this then your truth-seeking will end. You should throw away such phenomena and not cling to them during your practice.

After six at night there is strong concentration. My concentration is good at this time almost every day.

I was surely doing well in meditation at night. Though there is a difference in every person, my own concentration was good soon after sunset.

There was a repeated phenomenon that breathing would change by itself and my body would feel shock; my breath dwindled until it disappeared. Later the breath passed into my abdomen and I felt vibration all over my body. The sense, like pain, was almost noted and thoughts arising sometimes could

be noted.

What had been felt as defilements before changed now to thoughts. Consciousness comes to be changed by itself. This is profound and mysterious, therefore you cannot cheat. Consciousness can be expressed to the degree that it grows. The words of the enlightened are very simple and clear. The truth is simple and clear, and so there is no need of fancy words like those of Osho Rajneesh. If you read Buddhist Sutra, there are many fancy words. Those are not the sayings of Buddha. Buddha could not say such fancy words because of his purity. Likewise, neither can the enlightened. He uses simple words that can be understood by anybody.

Nov. 21, 1998

I felt very peaceful and calm in a state of concentration. It came about by itself that breathing was very thin, with my body shocked, vibrating, and shaking, and my backbone straight. The pain and numbness was almost not felt as time passed. It was seen that there were many arising-vanishing within a breathing in and also within a breathing out. Breathing surely becomes thinner, almost not felt as the mind becomes calm. Can I say this is breathing?

Nov. 22, 1998

After the Dharma talk, I spoke with a monk from Korea about Mahayana and Theravada Buddhism. It was a good oppor-

tunity to learn about the differences in the doctrines, but I thought both of them have completely lost the fundamentals.

It is said that the Buddhism of southern Asia is Theravada and that of northern Asia is Mahayana. The monk from Korea said the Theravada monk is lower than the Mahayana; Mahayana monks live together with sentient beings by Buddha's compassion. This seemed to be the case. But I figured there was no difference between Mahayana and Theravada from the perspective of Buddha's enlightenment. Those concepts came up 500 to 1000 years after Buddha's death. It was ridiculous that people were arguing over doctrines such as Mahayana or Theravada and the right or wrong path, etc.

My practicing was not proceeding well from six o'clock that evening. Maybe the discussion about doctrine distracted my mind.

I felt painfully that keeping silence was so very important for practicing. My mind already seemed loose.

When there was otherwise calm and no thoughts arising in my mind during practice, if I had had a discussion with someone then those thoughts would continuously come up during meditation. So the whole day's practice became spoiled.

Nov. 24, 1998

We were going to move to the Chamoe Meditation Center, and in the process of paying a visit I bought a carved wooden sculpture at a downtown shopping mall.

I bought a carved statue without thinking because it seemed to have beautifully curved lines when I saw it in the store. But looking at it back at my residence I was suddenly surprised: it was a depiction of a man and woman hugging and kissing. Immediately my feeling for the statue died. I got angry, thinking, "I came here to become enlightened, what I am doing now? Why did I carelessly buy such a stupid sculpture? I wrapped it in a newspaper and tossed it into the corner. A few days later I went to the store to exchange it but was refused, and had to come back. I was angry, saying, "What nonsense is this?"

It was, in a word, pathetic. I was supposed to move to the Chamoe Meditation Center due to the big annual event, but we could not go because Sayadaw had already left on overseas travel. Under these circumstances, what a silly mistake to buy such a thing! As I was looking at the statue on the table without thinking, I felt something was wrong; there arose a thought, "It is only a wood carving, why are you so angry about it?" On reflection, it was ridiculous that I got angry at a sculpture even though I came here to practice Vipassana to remove such discrimination of being *sacred and unsacred.*

Suddenly I noted that I still had dualistic discrimination. I seemed to have been brainwashed with the notion that a seeker has to keep away from sex. Therefore in my subconscious there was the notion that I should not see such a sculpture. After noting this, I could look at the statue again. "It is just a piece of wood. Even if I see a man and woman hugging, what is wrong with that? Why do people think sex is vulgar?" These thoughts arose in succession. I noted, "Because I thought of sex as vulgar,

I was thus angry at seeing the sculpture."

Thinking, "This sculpture is not in my hand by accident. I will make working use of it," I put it again on the table and a photo of Buddha next to it. From time to time I would look at the wood carving and the photo of Buddha in turn. At first I felt uncomfortable, but later I got more comfortable, thinking, "What is the difference between Buddha and people having sex?"

I came to see no discrimination between them. I could see correctly that humans had been discriminating through having been brainwashed in dualistic discrimination: This is sacred, that is vulgar.

Thanks to the wood sculpture, such dualistic discrimination in my mind fell away. It also broke down the concept that Buddha is sacred. Strange to say, if I had exchanged it for another one, then I would not have realized that. But the seller refused. Therefore it was so profound and mysterious. There came up various means to help me on my path; when listening to a Dharma talk by a young monk, my ego broke down, and when seeing the wood carving, dualistic discrimination fell away from me.

Nov. 25, 1998

The peaceful mind kept its intensity, and dualistic discrimination over what is sacred or vulgar fell away from me. However, there arose an unprecedented phenomenon of many sad feelings.

These days I felt sad over everything: whenever seeing a suntanned girl or an old man carrying bricks, ants lining up to go diligently somewhere to find food, a mosquito sucking my blood, myself sitting all day long for nirvana, thinking of my family at home, and that I had no plan to live in the future. I felt comfortable before because I had an indefinite plan to live without thinking, but now I feel fearful; to live recklessly seems meaningless.

The mind is very strange. I thought before, "It is good just to live peacefully and die," but now it was impossible for me to do anything or to have any plan. But in reaction to that, suddenly there arose a thought, "I have not saved much money; how will my family live?" It was because of ego; a feeling of being afraid to go on living while feeling sad about everything. Then, observing, "What are these phenomena?" I knew that it was a sense of futility occurring as a result of the weakening ego. Because an ego has no more power, it arms itself with sadness to shake the mind.

Nov. 26, 1998

Due to the annual event, the setting became distracted with people moving to other places.

Now I gave up the idea of moving from the center, thinking, "I actually came here on a one-year plan, so the place being noisy just for two weeks will not be so important. This will be a good opportunity for my practice." But I was a bit distracted even just from needing to move rooms in the center. At that time, something funny occurred.

I felt bad that somebody was using my soap improperly in the shower room, so I brought it back to my room. After a later realization, I felt strongly that ego was attacking me in this minute way.

Though this is shameful for a seeker, I am telling you about it. To be a seeker, I had given up working at a company for a salary, yet I got angry about somebody using a cheap bar of soap. After carrying it to my room, I noted that I could not forgive myself being angry at such a small thing, yet forgiving myself over larger matters. For a single piece of soap I got completely distracted. Actually this kind of thing becomes a good opportunity for work; ego would attack me by various means, both weak and strong.

Nov. 27, 1998

Because appearing-disappearing is going on whenever a breath arises and vanishes, there comes a birth-death every moment. Therefore there is no same existence from moment to moment. While walking in meditation, I felt that the movement of my steps was like the wind.

I felt my body weightless like the wind while walking in meditation; there was a little progress in my practice. Being angry about soap meant that ego was showing its last defense; here is the matter of life or death to the ego.

Ego wanted to make me give up enlightenment, because

once I become enlightened the ego would die. So it tried to control me by various means. Here is Old, saying, "If the degree of Tao [the path] is high, then that of Mara [the demon] is also high." It means that good always comes with bad. Moreover, a small disturbance can be more dangerous than a big one. Therefore if one surrenders after such a trivial event, it means that the path of awakening would be completely blocked. However, while practicing in meditation, I came to be sharply mindful; I felt my step softly while walking in meditation.

In making acute observation of the breath, I noted, "rising, falling, sitting" in three steps instead of "rising, falling" in two steps.

If observation becomes close, concentration will be stronger, without boredom, noting more acutely by observing more variously.

Nov. 28, 1998

While sitting in meditation, there is feeling from the breathing body and the mind cognizing it. While walking, there is feeling from the foot contacting the ground and the mind cognizing it; likewise there should be "consciousness" to note seeing, hearing, smelling, tasting, feeling, and thinking. What is the consciousness cognizing?

There arose a question. It was clear that consciousness takes note, but who or what is the consciousness that is cognizing? That was the one last question for me. That was pure consciousness. However, one mistakenly believes one's self to be that consciousness, identifying oneself with seeing, hearing, tasting, feeling, thinking, and touching. Consciousness is pure consciousness itself projected from true nature; pure consciousness manifests itself into many forms with which one mistakenly identifies oneself as an independent individual.

As a metaphorical example, when we dream, there is always "I" in that dream, along with many other people. But in a dream only one is cognized as "I," not the others. However, after dreaming, I can wonder who it was that made me think, say, act in the dream? It was consciousness. And then who was it that made the others think, say, act in the dream? It was also consciousness. Simply speaking, the consciousness that dreams is giving its own consciousness to "I" as well as to the others in the dream. Whatever I and the others in a dream speak, think, and act is all different; each thinks of themselves as doing, but that is misidentification.

The manifested world is the same as the dreamed one. Because we are in a dream of the manifested world, we perceive that *I* and *you* are all different in saying, thinking, and acting. However, let this world be a dream and therefore let us turn to the consciousness. This consciousness is assigning roles to all entities. Because we are stuck in a dream, we mistakenly identify ourselves with these roles assigned by the scenario. At that time my practice was blocked by this question. There was no one to answer it. It may be very easy to understand for you because I am explaining it in detail. Be sure that you keep in mind what I said and finally have it melt down from your head into your heart; you should keep it at the center of your heart. Then you can never identify yourself with others. If you keep it just in your head as knowledge, it will be changed into ego whenever you confront problems.

While sitting and noting "rising, falling, sitting," I felt my body as no more mine. My breathing stopped and I noted my body as a being in itself.
From that time did I begin to vaguely feel myself as a being rather than any individual entity.

I noted that so many thoughts arising about past, present, future all passed away in a moment.
When we think, there are many thoughts that arise and vanish in a moment. If our mindfulness becomes strong, we note that those thoughts really flash up and disappear in a moment. Even before being enlightened, we can note this if some progress in meditation had been made; all things appear and disappear in a moment. Therefore attachments fall away to some degree. Only no-self is not yet realized. However if such noting becomes strong and acute, no-self cannot but be realized. What if a fruit is ripe enough? It will drop by itself. That is the truth.

I noted that body-mind and the manifested universe are all nothing but a continuum of arising and passing away.
I began to know what birth and death really mean.

Prior to all behavior there must come intention, and then is it

not no-I? That means, is there "I" having an intention to do?
There arose another question. From the last threshold of no-I frequently arose such a question. Intention is another expression of a thought. Though every day I muttered to myself, "Thoughts, words, and activities arising in my body and mind are not caused by "I" but manifested by themselves by dependent origination," if there was a little change of just one word in it, I became confused.

Nov. 30, 1998
When changing from walking to sitting or vice versa, noting continued clearly due to moving slowly.
When changing posture in meditation, I would usually become distracted from noting. Therefore *samathi* and noting did not continue. Therefore I noted every movement and stood up very slowly after sitting: putting right hand, putting left hand, lifting hip, left step, right step, etc. When changing from walking to sitting, I also noted as such and started to observe breathing. If practicing likewise for a few hours, then mindfulness began to strengthen faster.

Dec. 1, 1998
The mind intending, acting, and noting it all arise and vanish at the same time. Even the mind cognizing the phenomenon of arising-vanishing should disappear. There is nothing permanent.

Now I came to note that the manifested universe is impermanence itself because of the continuum of all things arising-vanishing, arising-vanishing.

Dec. 2, 1998

From waking up from sleep, samathi kept occurring. Though there was a loud noise from the speaker and many people were walking around the center due to the annual event, my mind was calm and clear.

The annual event at the center began on November 30. Though I stayed in the noisy and crowded surroundings, I was rather absorbed in *samathi* from that time. In spite of such conditions, nothing disturbed me. Such a state of *samathi* within me continued for a week.

It seems good that I have more time to read and meditate according to my own schedule for a week. These days whenever I read a book, tears fall from my eyes because I feel such beauty in the truth.

As happened when seeing something like ants before, now when reading the books of Maharaj and Maharshi, I felt in them such beauty from the simple and clear expressions of the truth that it made tears flow from my eyes.

Dec. 3, 1998

When reading Pointers from Nisargadatta Maharaj, I felt the ego disappearing as my heart was all cleared, as if a rope were suddenly cut. I realized, "This should be no-I. Though there is not I originally, I have tried to become the Buddha by cultivating the body-mind with which I identify myself. What a comedy!"

I had brought three books to Myanmar: *Pointers from Nisargadatta Maharaj*, *Who am I?* by Ramana Maharshi, and a book about Vipassana meditation. At that time, while reading *Pointers from Nisargadatta Maharaj*, I remained in a state of *samathi*. In spite of it being so noisy outside, these sentences touched my heart like jewels in a calm and peaceful state without any disturbances. While staying in this state, my heart was all cleared by this paragraph:

What causes bondage is identification resulting in the imagined concept of an independent, autonomous entity, which assumes the doer-ship and thus takes delivery of the actions and the responsibility for the consequences.

Though I have read this book many times, this time I felt my heart all cleared while reading this paragraph. However, do you also feel likewise? I am going to explain to you why my heart was cleared.

The self-identification with the body results in "the imagined doer"; a doer, an ego, does not exist in reality but only as an imagined concept. This imagined pseudo-entity behaves as a doer—"I did this"—I thought, I said, I acted. Why can the imagined entity not exist independently? Because it is a relative being manifested in the relative world. The imagined concept means emptiness, illusion. Taking "delivery of the actions and the responsibility for the consequences" is the cause of bondage. But if you do not do so, what will happen? It means there is no bondage. It is simple: do not take responsibility regardless of what you do. Why? Because there is no-responsibility.

But people misuse the idea of "no-responsibility," as if they are not responsible for something. No-responsibility means that there does not exist such a responsibility. Because of no-I (no-self), there is no responsibility. Is there karma? No. Because of no-I, there is no karma. Is there rebirth? No. Because of no-karma, there is no rebirth. Why do you take responsibility for the consequences? Originally there is no-responsibility. What are the horrible events that happen? They are part of a scenario. Did an actor who committed robbery in a play feel guilty and go to jail in reality? On seeing this paragraph my heart was all cleared, and so now I am free from bondage.

From that day I stopped practicing meditation. There was no need for practice, for having realized no-I (no-self), the purpose of practice disappeared. This is called *don-oh-don-soo*; being enlightened, spiritual practice finishes immediately. Why? Because of self-identification, I began to practice but "I" disappeared. Then who is it who will practice? Therefore practicing has to finish. How easy it would be if realization came up all at once. But it did not do so. Because self-identification over a long period was so strong, there were wanderings in spite of the realization; after a week my heart became unclear again. If there had been an enlightened master around at that time, I could have asked for advice and would not have been so surprised at it.

At that time a young monk from Korea died in a car accident, so there was a cremation funeral service for him. It was another good opportunity for my practice. Looking at the burning body on fire, I thought, "Who is dead?" There is no-I, yet people were saying, "What a pity that a young monk died." Who was that body on fire? It was just a dream. There was a dead man in a dream. There is no one dead. But in a dream they burn the one that died and cry. However, in reality nobody was dead. You should understand this correctly; there is no come and go, never born and died. Because everything is all a dream, there is no one born and died, and no event.

Dec. 12, 1998

I am in big trouble. I do not know what to do because the feeling of no-I suddenly disappeared. And also there is no more progress in observation and concentration. I feel pressure on my chest.

I went back to the beginning. The feeling of no-I disappeared. I still knew that there was no-I, but the clear and vivid feeling of no-I as if a rope had been cut was being blocked again after a week. "There is no-I, so what?" Therefore I read Maharaj's book again. I read it throughout to find the feeling again but failed. Was I embarrassed! Surely I realized no-I, but my heart had become blocked up again in a week.

So I read the book twice but could not find the feeling. But when I read the book by Maharshi, there was a paragraph to console me, an answer to the question: "When a complete no-I comes up, that is complete enlightenment. But such a state of enlightenment comes up several times." I thought, "The realization of no-I cannot be attained at once, due to lifelong habits." I found comfort in that paragraph. If not I might have been so very confused. It was the first time for me and so I could not know it. The master was needed for spiritual practice. He will provide a check as to whether the disciples' practice is going well or not. Because there was no master for me at that time, it made me almost go crazy. There was no one to consult. Even my meditation practice was not going well. Deciding, "Let's start all over again," I began practicing Vipassana again.

Once I fell, it continued to go badly despite starting over again. When walking in meditation I stopped near a window to look through it at a passing woman; naturally my eyes followed her to watch her hips in her tight-fitting dress. There arose in me a bit of sexual desire. While I was at a loss what to do because the feeling of enlightenment had disappeared, moreover there had now arisen a sexual desire. I fell on the floor, saying, "What is wrong with me? A sexual desire arose in me! Now all that is over." Everything I had done until that moment felt absurd, messed up.

Then while I sat vacantly, there came a question, "From whom is this frustration arising?" Then upon reflecting further, in a moment there arose a thought: "This body-mind is not 'I' and a sexual desire arose by itself in the mind, but due to identifying myself with the body-mind that raised the sexual desire, there came frustration." At that moment, suddenly there came the second enlightenment in me, "Ah! There should be no-I, but I had lost it and had been deluded again!" This time the feeling of enlightenment was stronger than before, because of having lost it once.

Let us summarize again. When seeing a woman, there arose a sexual desire and then frustration in response. "Why did the frustration arise?" Because of a thought, "I created the sexual desire." However, soon the next question in the chain came, "Who is frustrated?" This turned the issue around in the opposite direction. Therefore, if the Vipassana meditation practice goes well, there arises a power from within, despite the frustration. That is why meditation is necessary. Though meditation seems not to go well, this power comes when necessary. Likewise, all that had been cleared and the realization of no-I returned: "This body-mind is not 'I,' but frustration followed because I identified myself with the one causing a sexual desire even though it arose in the mind." From this second realization of no-I, I have never again lost it.

There were two occasions of realization for me. From that time there came to me a complete enlightenment of no-I. Though there can arise something in the mind or some actions in the body, those all occur by themselves according to the scenario, not caused by ourselves as independent individuals. We can say that those are done by dependent origination on the phenomenal side. Simply speaking, those are done by the law of *paticca-samuppada* in Buddhism. The fact you meet me here is not by your own choice but by the scenario. You became a seeker by scenario not by your interest in the truth. All things are flowing now according to dependent origination.

Although I mistakenly thought of something chosen, planned, and done by me, that was not done by me. It is fully correct. You should always remember this point. The thought that "I have done" is all just delusion. It is also a delusion that all living beings not enlightened are trapped in the circle of rebirth but the enlightened are not. Is the delusion reborn? Where does the delusion arise from? It arose from the mind; if there is no body-mind, the delusion will disappear simultaneously. Once no-I is realized, then the other questions shall be so automatically.

Dec. 17, 1998

Though sexual desire and frustration are just phenomena arising and vanishing in the mind, I mistakenly identified myself with this body-mind for a moment, but there is no I as a subject who raised sexual desire and frustration.

Dec. 19, 1998

When I woke up early in the morning, everything was clear. The identification with this body-mind is completely cut off and never comes up. It is so surprising that I could not see such a clear and simple understanding until now. Such a feeling passed away from me two weeks ago and now there is no hindrance to me anymore. There is just a phenomenon of awakening, but it is not I who awakens; there is only arising, but it is not I who arise.

Now all things within and without are seen as phenomena, as they are.

Dec. 20, 1998

When standing up after sitting meditation I felt dizzy. The dizziness did not happen to me, because there was no-I, with just clear phenomena and mindfulness. Now I keep being mindful of no-I. While sitting and observing thoughts arising, I noted that they arise and disappear by themselves according to dependent origination, because there is no subject to think.

Dec. 22, 1998

After taking a shower and reading a book, I felt tired and fell asleep on the bed while noting. However, at the moment of waking up I noted that I was waking in a state of samathi. There was clearly only the phenomenon of waking but not I who woke up. After a while I noted the opening of the eyes, another phenomenon, more clearly, but still not I. All thoughts and actions were seen just as phenomena and there was not 'I' as a doer anywhere. The manifested world, including this body-mind, is only full of phenomena arising and passing away.

Dec. 23, 1998

I awoke from a dream last night soon after noting, "There is no-I." Now that everything is cognized as a clear phenomenon from the moment of waking up, there is no subjective entity to think and act.

When realizing no-I the first time, I felt it becoming unclear over time, whereas when the second realization came, the feeling of no-I sharpened and became clearer as time passed; it continued in dreaming as "there is no-self." Consciousness becomes likewise in reality. In dreaming I do this or that and it is over at the moment of waking up; there is nothing left. It is identical in daily life. Sometimes you remember something but it is just remembrance without any attachment. It is nothing but a notice for consciousness, because every thought and action arising in the body-mind occurs through dependent origination.

Just observe! Pure consciousness is watching all things just as they are—but if it becomes an individual, it will cling to things arising in the body-mind. This is a difference. Nobody, even the Buddha, could change events, thoughts, words, and actions arising in the body-mind; those are just flowing according to the given scenario. Only the enlightened do not identify themself with phenomena arising in the body-mind; there is no mistaken thinking that "I did it," whereas the unenlightened may know intellectually "this body-mind is not I," but when meeting a real situation, they come to mistakenly think, "I did it." There is not much difference between them; it is only whether or not the person becomes deluded.

The teachings of Sakyamuni Buddha have not been passed on correctly. The Buddha said that his teachings would continue only until 500 years after his death and then there would be no more truth; the true meaning of his teachings would be distorted. Yes, his prediction came true. The Buddha's enlightenment is of dependent origination with no-self; all beings in the manifested world are relative, dependent ones, and so nobody can be born by themselves alone. Because of being born by dependent origination, there is not a self, not a subject. Therefore, dependent origination and no-self are one and cannot be separated. And there is no rebirth because of no-self. Now, however, what is Buddhism saying, both about dependent origination and rebirth? No, those two cannot co-exist; if there is a self to be reborn, then how can there be no-self?

The Buddha talked about dependent origination, upsetting the thought of rebirth, India's Brahmanism at the time. However, Buddhism is now affirming rebirth again, and what happened? Buddhism overturned again the Buddha's thoughts of dependent origination that had upset the thought of rebirth after his enlightenment. It went back to a state of ignorance. They are saying, merely as a phrase, "Buddha realized the dependent origination with no-I," but have divided it into twelve stages, explaining this as the process of individual rebirth. They made it into a distorted doctrine. There is no such thing. The truth is simple. Independent origination cannot be divided into twelve stages, nor can there be enlightenment of the seventh or eighth stage, etc.

Dec. 26, 1998

In a dream a beautiful angel said that she wanted to sleep with me and we had sex. I woke up realizing I had experienced a wet dream. Though my underpants were soaked, I never felt unpleasant, just noting it as a physiological phenomenon arising naturally in this body-mind. After taking a shower, I went to bed again.

This was a highlight. Do the enlightened have wet dreams? This alters the perception of the world. Do not think of the enlightened in such fantasy. Because people are in attendance to the Sakyamuni Buddha as a holy image plated with gold, they think this should be a standard of the enlightened. They cannot be enlightened thinking this way. Did the Buddha live without taking a shit? You should not believe this.

One day, Seo Jung-joo visited with Ven. Seong-chul, a zen master, to ask him, "Venerable one, though I am almost sixty years old, when I see a beautiful woman I feel sexual desire. What the hell is this? How about you?" The monk said, "So that is why the monks pray, read scriptures, and meditate every day." Both should have been very honest men, but it is a problem that they think of sexual desire as bad, something to overcome. Most monks are now stuck in this pattern. They see sex as something impure and thus as a kind of hindrance to overcome in order to be enlightened. Who shall overcome what?

For example, in an old story there were a man and a woman, both sensual beings. People considered them sinners and bad people, and they felt guilty about being born that way. Therefore the woman felt distressed enough to visit the priest and confess her sin. "Father, I was born as a sensual woman and if I see a handsome man, I just lie on the ground. What shall I do?" The priest said, "Please chant the Lord's Prayer a hundred times and then don't worry." Then she visited the monk with the same confession and he said, "Please bow to the Buddha three thousand times." If she had gone to a counselor, he might say, "Take a cold shower whenever sexual desire arises, then it shall pass."

If she came to me, what would I say? "Never worry about it and do as much as you want." The body-mind shall move according to the scenario given. Because thinking by dualistic discrimination of the body-mind as "myself" and of sex as vulgar, I will suffer torment. We do not need it, so why should we suffer? The one who has assumed a role as a prostitute in a scenario has to do her role. Can a prostitute assigned by scenario perform the role of Mother Teresa if she tries hard? People's dualistic discrimination increases the suffering of others. They are suffering themselves and also causing it for others. A life is to live as given; we have to live with no-I. Nobody can escape from the role assigned. Someone gets married five or six times. Is it so because they want to do this? It is because of the scenario, so what can they do?

In theory, you might seem to accept all this but if in a real situation, then you might say, "But it will be difficult to do that because we should save face in life." However, all things are bound to flow as assigned in the scenario. You should not identify yourself with this body-mind. It shall do everything its role has assigned. Therefore you should not suffer. Why do you want to be responsible? You are not responsible. So live a comfortable life. You think, "There is no responsibility, so I will do what I like from today," but that is impossible. You can do as much as your role has been assigned in the scenario. Live a free life; true freedom shall come to you when you put everything down. Live a life freely as the role assigned, as it is. When something comes up, what will you do? Everything will be fine, but only if there is no thought of "I did it".

Maharaj said, "Even if you killed someone, it will be good if you do not have the thought of 'I killed.'" But if one who thinks of this body-mind as himself killed someone, then how can he not take on the thought of killing? Do the enlightened teach something untrue? It is so because there is no-I. Though you are not enlightened yet, do not discriminate against what you did nor what others did. If you keep on doing so, you will naturally come later not to discriminate. You should not discriminate even against yourself for doing so. There is nothing for me to do, and how comfortable it is! And then everything will go on by itself.

You have to keep practicing Vipassana meditation. You will know its power when feeling serious frustration; if you have the power of Vipassana within, then it comes up to overcome the frustration. However, one who is usually not mindful will come to wander around if frustrated, or fall into nihilism. Though I explain the truth in general terms, it is you who have to realize the truth in the long run. In order to realize it, there is no way other than noting it as it is, so you have to keep observing and noting.

Therefore I am revealing to you that I practiced the meditation of mindfulness. There is no other way. Maharaj also kept practicing for the truth taught by his master for three years while running a cigar store. He kept observing and noting the mind for three years and then became enlightened at 37 years old. He had dropped out of primary school in the fourth year. He had not learned much and was an old hand at physical labor. He became enlightened because of his purity. As I have always told you, you have to harmoniously keep the three characteristics of the seeker: purity, sincerity, patience. Among those, purity is the most important.

Verification of Enlightenment

Staying at the meditation center for ten days more after this, I compared and tested my enlightenment to be exactly the same as that of Buddha, Maharshi, and Maharaj. Let me briefly talk about my notes summarizing the truth at that time.

Buddha's teaching, represented by the vastness of the Tripitaka Koreana (eighty thousand scriptures of Buddhism), is unexpectedly very simple. The key point of the three Dharma characteristics is no-self. There is no-self in every existence of the manifested world. Because there are no permanent beings, all things have to exist in mutually dependent change. It means to exist by dependent origination; by this arising does that arise, by that existing does this exist. Therefore if this disappears, that also disappears automatically, and if this does not exist, then that also does not exist. However, because a being itself can exist only relatively, there must relatively appear opposite concepts, such as you-me, good-evil, thing-nothing, and pain-pleasure etc. This included the identification of myself with the body-mind due to thinking of myself as an individual entity in the process of manifestation.

The thought of "I am," the first delusion, forms an ego, the basic ignorance that causes the identification of "myself" with all phenomena arising in the body-mind, and this brings suffering. Therefore the world becomes a furnace of suffering because desire, grasping, and dualistic discrimination continue to become stronger. The sentient beings who become slaves of ego are suffering from their desires and attachments because of identifying themselves with the body-mind, and they cannot be free due to wandering around in the endless pit of relative concepts.

Then what if you realize the simple fact that there does not exist a subject as "I"? The ego will disappear and you can see that the body-mind and all things in the manifested world are simply continuing phenomena arising and passing away by the law of dependent origination.

Though seeing leaves falling down with no-mind, sentient beings cannot see the body-mind with no-mind. Therefore, if there is no self-identification with an existence of an individual entity, existence itself becomes no-self by dependent origination, therefore there is no dualistic discrimination: that is the middle path. Because of no-self, there is no birth-death, no good-evil, or joy-sorrow. If there is no dualistic discrimination, then both extremes, relative concepts, come to exist together. It is the middle way—the form is the emptiness, the emptiness is the form. This truth is to explain only "no-self, originally no-I," that is "the Absolute, the true nature," according to Maharaj.

If you realize only this, the Tripitaka Koreana is useless, just an expedient. It is because too many doctrines shackle the seekers. Right now, most seekers are trying to cultivate their bodies and minds in order to become Buddha, a holy being; trying to make no-self by removing the ego. And so they think that they have to develop *samathi* to keep awake day and night, to realize the state of extinguishing the mind and becoming Buddha. Who can keep awake day and night, realize the state of extinguishing their mind, and become Buddha?

That first view of truth is wrong. Though one might practice like this for decades, one cannot be enlightened. Buddha is not a holy and great person.

It is Buddha who realizes that there is no "I" originally, that such desire, attachment, and dualistic discrimination are not actions done by the self, and who will be never deluded again.

This is the truth that all enlightened have conveyed. The truth cannot be attained nor created. If you can really wake up from the first delusion that there is no-self originally, there is nothing more to realize or cultivate.

"No-self" means to realize that there is originally no-I as an independent individual entity, not to reach somewhere by getting rid of an existing ego. Like the saying, "Everything depends on the mind," the mind can do anything and thus make everything very complicated for itself. However, if you notice that there is no root, no subject in all such complicated things, then defilements will disappear all at once.

One day, zen master Huiyang met zen master Mazo in meditation and asked, "What are you doing now?"

Mazo said, "I am practicing meditation to become Buddha."

Hearing that, Huiyang brought a broken roof tile, sat beside him and started polishing it. Mazo thought this very strange and asked, "What are you doing now?"

He said, "I am going to polish this roof tile and make it into a mirror."

It is equally mindless behavior to polish a roof file into a mirror as it is to cultivate one's mind to become Buddha. Of course, the mind has to be calm to realize true nature; just as a thing in boiling water cannot be seen as it is, but it can be seen in calm water. As long as one's mind reaches out to cling to or discriminate against anything, one can never realize true nature. Therefore it is a spiritual practice that one turns one's mind to the inner side. And then one can note "no-self," the true nature to realize the middle path. It is an expedient, not a purpose for enlightenment to remove the three poisons (desire, anger, ignorance) by morality, concentration, and wisdom. Once one realizes "no-self," one comes to note that there are no such poisons to be removed, and no birth-death, sacred-vulgar, joy-sorrow to be overcome. All things are just byproducts arising from the ego, the delusion of "I." There is only seeing the false as false and the truth as true; there are no stages it is necessary to take.

In Buddhism there has been a continuous argument over *don-oh-don-soo* and *don-oh-jeom-soo,* the relationship between cultivation and enlightenment. *Don-oh-jeom-soo* (immediate awakening and then gradual cultivation) is an opinion from acquaintance with but not full understanding of enlightenment. If there remain old habits to be cultivated, then it means that there still remains an ego and so no-self is not yet realized. Therefore it is a wrong argument, from regarding "understanding the truth through knowledge" as enlightenment. If realizing no-self then it becomes a state of nirvana with an ego no longer existing. Why is cultivation needed? When mistakenly thinking that there still remains an ego, one needs cultivation. However, after realizing that originally such ego does not exist, one does not need it. Therefore *don-oh-don-soo* is the right argument; when enlightened, cultivation is finished simultaneously. Enlightenment is a mere appearance of true nature as it is, not something new to cultivate and attain. And so such debate is just arguments among sentient beings, but originally there is neither enlightenment nor cultivation.

Therefore there is no enlightenment, nor nirvana. If there is no dualistic discrimination, then everything becomes truth as it is. Because the whole phenomenal universe exists with dependent origination and without independent entities, everything is originally no-self and exists harmoniously along the middle path without dualistic discrimination. Because of no-self, to Buddha all things are seen as one, but to sentient beings who do not know no-self as independent individual entities the ego appears to continuously cause desire, attachment, and dualistic discrimination. The enlightened note that karma is also just cause-and-effect by dependent origination and originally there is no subject to cause karma or any independent self to receive it. This is nirvana. However, because sentient beings believe that there is self, they mistakenly identify themselves with the words, thoughts, and actions arising in their body-mind, and thus suffer. Therefore, karma becomes a law of individual fate, not one of natural dependent origination, in which an ego causes a desire of existence and makes one become a slave of one's body-mind.

Why can some seekers not be enlightened? There are a few important misidentifications.

First, they think of 'no-self' as a stage to attain by removing the existing ego. However, originally there is no independent self, no ego.

Second, they think of 'Buddha' as a sacred stage to reach through cultivating the body-mind and getting rid of desire, anger, and ignorance. Buddha, or sentient beings, comes from the dualistic discrimination arising in delusion, but there is no-self, so who is Buddha? Who is a sentient being? If dualistic discrimination is disconnected, a sentient being is Buddha just as they are. Because there is not a sentient being separately, all are originally Buddha. Therefore neither the enlightened nor the sentient being is a dependent individual entity. One only thinks of oneself as a dependent individual mistakenly.

Third, they are bound by expedients. Once stepping into the world of the spirit, they become unwittingly brainwashed by religious tradition, group, custom, blind faith, etc. They do not know how highly addictive those are. Most of them are too addictive to get out of. Christianity became addicted to Jesus, Buddhists to Buddha, zen masters to *hua-tou* and yogis to yoga. Likewise they become so easily addicted to their teachers, groups, and performances that they could not see other things with an equal view.

Blind faith exists not only in pseudo-religion, claiming a leader as the savior, but also in any religious group. Such a narrow-minded attitude should not be held by a seeker. This is brainwashing, which we fear because it causes an addiction to take root without our knowledge. The Buddha knew such an addiction well and said, "Do not depend on me and do not cling to anything because they are just expedients for enlightenment."

One of the important things that I realized within a month after starting practice in Vipassana meditation was to successfully overcome religious self-righteousness and the addiction painfully experienced while joining many Eastern and Western religious groups. Because of such experiences, I could accept equally and realize the teachings of all the enlightened ones.

Looking back on my path of seeking truth, everyone and every event were my masters, but it was Maharshi, Maharaj, and the Buddha who had decisive influence on my enlightenment. You might ask why I had so many masters, but I had to accept the diversity of masters because there was no one master who transferred enlightenment to me directly. The teaching of Maharshi was like a telescope to bring me closer to the truth felt far away, and that of Maharaj was like a microscope to let me observe the truth minutely, while the Vipassana of the Buddha was the practice for me to realize no-self directly.

However, what is more important is not to be attached to anything. If one is attached to religion, knowledge, or practice, then the ego only gets stronger and harder, whereas enlightenment becomes farther away. If I had only read the book of Maharshi or Maharaj without practicing in Vipassana, then I surely could not have gotten what I needed; if I had only practiced in Vipassana without knowing Maharshi and Maharaj, then I would have been just wasting time acquiring techniques of meditation. The teachings of Buddhism are too vast and can in fact be a hindrance to understanding the simple truth.

That means that the truth taught by the Buddha has been distorted.

Now let us explore a few important teachings of Maharshi and Maharaj:

> "The enlightened knows that he is not the body and thus not doing anything even when the body is carrying out actions."
>
> "If there arise some thoughts, 'I-notion' arises like a host of the thoughts: "I think," "I believe," "I want," "I am doing." However, in fact, there is no I-notion existing independently without identifying with the objects. The reason why the I-notion keeps arising like a reality is that the identification is continuing."
>
> "The important thing is that although doing something, you have to get out of the feeling I am doing the action. The feeling of myself doing it is the bondage."
>
> "It is the problem that a person thinks himself a doer. However, it is misunderstanding. Every action is done by the stronger power and the human is just an instrument." *(Maharshi)*
>
> "Functioning of manifestation takes place so long as there is consciousness. By unnecessarily identifying one-

self as the doer one attracts responsibility and guilt."

"You are—you have always been—where you want to be led. Actually, there really is no 'where' that you can be led to. The answer is just a perception; nothing to be done. There must be a total absence of the 'doer,' the total absence of both the positive and negative aspects of 'doing.' Indeed, this is true surrender."

"A mere object, an appearance—which is all that a physical body is—cannot possibly perform any action whatsoever as an independent entity? It is only when the Impersonal Consciousness, in its total functioning, manifests by objectifying itself and becomes identified with each object that the concept of the personal I comes into being. This concept is the source of bondage, the objectivizing of I, the pure subjectivity, into an objective me. It is this me—the I-concept, or the ego—which is the imaginary bondage from which liberation is sought. A clear perception of what constitutes the sentient being that is seeking liberation will show how ludicrous the whole idea is."

"Stand back in your original state of wholeness, the state before you were 'born,' when there was no knowledge I am and, therefore, no need and want of any kind. All suffering will end as soon as you stand apart in pure awareness of the false as false, the transient as transient."

(Maharaj)

The truth is thus simple. But the human mind is complicated. The source of this mind is the I-notion, the ego. There is originally no-ego, no-I as an individual entity but only a delusion. If one does not identify oneself with any thought and action arising, there is no attachment, responsibility, or suffering. However, it does not mean that one should blindly believe "no-I." Because it is as good as saying that you will be saved only by believing in Jesus Christ. Buddha said: Observe and realize "no-I" through practice in Vipassana.

It is a greatness of Vipassana that one does not need to overcome the body-mind nor to remove the defilements, but just watch the phenomenon as it is without intervening. Therefore one has to realize how the whole manifested universe, including the body-mind, is impermanent, suffering and repeating birth-death without subjectivity by dependent origination. It is the sentient beings who think of no-existence as existence and are attached to something impossible. On the other hand, it is Buddha who sees the truth as truth, the false as false to know that there is essentially nothing to be attached to or discriminate against—no good-evil, no sacred-vulgar, no birth-death—and realizes that the truth is as it is, to be in the middle path without intervening or being affected. Buddha is the manifested phenomenon itself, not personality. Though the enlightened as a manifested phenomenon are each seen as individuals, Buddha exists only as one because of no division; me and you.

Sakyamuni, the Buddha, was born as prince of a country. However, he left his family and gave up his desire for pleasure to search for freedom from the defilements and suffering of birth, old age, sickness, and death, practiced asceticism and finally became the Buddha. It is possible only when one becomes completely free from the misunderstanding of the I-notion as an individual entity and the attachment to possessions that one is able to get the great freedom from suffering and greed arising, and the ego of thinking of oneself as the body-mind.

Sakyamuni, the Buddha, said, "It is nirvana to be a state of being in the middle path; no more dualistic discrimination, through realizing no-self." Buddha is the one who understood that there is originally not a self as an individual entity to realize the true nature, true-I. Only one like this shall be a really free person who lives a natural life beyond life-death and dualistic discrimination. However, it is easy for seekers to fall into many hindrances during practice. While going into deep practice and experiencing a temporary *samathi*, one sometimes comes to attain wisdom in a calm state. Here there are many seekers who believe that they are enlightened because of some new experience. All seekers come to experience this once or twice. Therefore if not in a state of no-I, being completely free from dualistic discrimination, then the ego comes to arise again.

Ultimate enlightenment means that the ego does not arise any more, just as the bucket with a broken rope can no longer come out of the well. If not in such a state, one does not yet become enlightened. It is just a state of experiencing temporary *samathi* through practice. Sakyamuni Buddha was not seduced by temporary *samathi* but kept on practicing to attain the ultimate "no-I" through the teachings of several gurus.

It is a pity that we could not easily find a real seeker in today's world. There are many people who, if they have a small experience as a result of practicing techniques, boast about it as if they were enlightened, deceiving people. The Buddha or the enlightened do not start to teach before realizing no-I, the ultimate enlightenment, and keep practicing as a seeker; they all started to teach as a master only after attaining the ultimate enlightenment. On the contrary, among those who acted as a master before being enlightened there is no one who has realized enlightenment before death. This is because the ego becomes strongest if pretending to be a master before being enlightened. The ego is very dangerous; even though one gives up everything to be a seeker, one can still unknowingly create attachments, make acquaintances, and maintain an ego.

On the other hand, there are many other seekers who devote themselves to practicing hard over decades, but why do they not become enlightened in spite of this?

It is impossible to realize "no-I" by cultivating the body-mind, because of misunderstanding the fundamental truth. It is natural that thoughts and actions continuously arise as long as one has breath. If not, one must be a corpse or a stone. If one has to throw away and overcome something to get the truth, then how could it be the truth? It is natural life and the nature of the free man who just watches thoughts and actions arising in the body-mind without ego, the notion of "I did," and sees all phenomena without dualistic discrimination.

The ignorant think of the enlightened as sacred, independent personalities. Although committing murder or adultery, Buddha never killed or committed adultery. The sentient beings are also the same. It is because there is only a doing, not a doer, due to no-I as an individual entity. Here, there again arise delusions for sentient beings:

"The sentient beings might do so, but how could the enlightened kill or commit adultery?"

The ignorance, the ego is arising based on the misidentification with the body. There is not "I" as a doer, whether one is Buddha or a sentient being. Although committing a murder, if there is no I-notion, there is no karma and no suffering. However, one cannot escape the defilement that the killer is oneself, before realizing no-I and the ego disappearing. This is the suffering of sentient beings, and the profound and mysterious harmony of the mind. Because the truth is beyond human common sense and thus too hard to understand, few have been enlightened since Sakyamuni, the Buddha.

After thus having investigated everything in detail, I silently left the beloved Mahashi Meditation Center after two months in the morning sunlight on January 1, 1999, at the beginning of a new year.

I was no longer a personality as an independent entity. Like all enlightened ones, I exist as true nature in whom the ego has disappeared leaving no dualistic discrimination. Therefore this body-mind called Haegong lives only as manifested true nature.

101 Wisdoms

Thoughts and actions are just the functioning of the body-mind mistakenly identified as "I," and true nature does not move.

Therefore true nature cannot be affected by any change of the manifested world, including the body-mind, and thus not by good or evil.

Enlightenment is that ignorance in the dark becoming one with the light of wisdom when the individual identity blocking it disappears.

Enlightenment is just to be manifested; an individual entity does not *become* enlightened. There is no Buddha, saint, or enlightened one. The thought that anyone is enlightened is delusion.

There has been no change since enlightenment was manifested to me.

Only the misidentification of myself with the body-mind has disappeared.

With any action, there is no suffering connected with it if one has no thought of oneself as a doer.

The enlightened one is not separate from the manifested

world because of being one with the truth, but the unenlightened one is separate from it because of being separated from the truth.

Enlightenment is possible only when one gives up trying to make an individual identity into a saint.

The unenlightened is someone who is suffering because their mind is always on the surface of the sea and facing the endless small or big waves. Conversely, the enlightened is the one who is just watching, with their mind always on a calm sea and so is never affected by any waves arising on the surface. The spiritual practitioner is one who sometimes goes into the sea to feel calm while staying on the surface, but faces rising waves due to the habituation of ego (tendency of mind).

If the ego blocking between body-mind and true nature disappears, the body-mind will be the manifestation of true nature because there is no bondage. However, it is not a permanent existence but is destined to appear and disappear.

Even if a terrible act, e.g. a murder, happens, do not identify yourself with that action and then there is no guilt and no suffering. Gradually you will see all thoughts and actions as they are.

The moment reality manifests itself, the Absolute becomes the relativity that is manifested as yin-yang, you-me. Relativity is a concept and an illusion due to being divided. The concept of pseudo-entity, "I—ego," may come up, and one comes to identify oneself with the body-mind (psychosomatic apparatus). However, the manifested is destined to disappear, and so however hard you try to let yourself exist continuously, you will have to pass away in the end.

Enlightenment is that wisdom which comes down to the heart from the head to go through the center of the being.

Generally we understand that habitual tendency is a habitual thought and an action of the body-mind. However, prior to it there is something fundamental that is not different from fundamental ignorance. Although understanding that the body-mind is not "I," when meeting objects of recognition one comes to identify oneself with the body-mind; that is the fundamental tendency of habit.

Because of there being no-I originally, there is a thought but no thinker, there is a word but no speaker, and there is an action but no doer.

The only practice that the seeker has to do is to give up everything unconditionally and then watch all phenomena arising and vanishing by themselves. However, do not cling even to watching. Because there is "I" watching. Keep in mind the fact that the deeper the practice gets, the stronger the ego can become.

I have three masters: Maharshi, Maharaj, and the Buddha. However, they are not three but one—true nature.

It is consciousness, not independent personality, that sees, hears, smells, tastes, thinks, speaks, and feels. Consciousness cannot be "I" because it does not have an individual entity. Therefore, an individual consciousness is an illusion created by the ego. It is only when pure consciousness manifests itself as an object that a personal consciousness appears to exist.

The birth-death that humans cling to are just phenomena that the body-mind temporarily arises and vanishes, not some subjective personality that is born and dies.

The further the consciousness is from pure consciousness, the closer it becomes to pure consciousness. Although consciousness has a tendency towards the outside, it shall go back to the inner side if it gets close to pure consciousness. When there arises a life event that makes consciousness turn to the inner side, then one comes to seek the truth. Because the seeker has already gone in the direction of true nature, they will experience no-self, even if at a different time.

There are only phenomena in this world. They cannot be divided like you and me, this and that. The saying, "In Buddha's eyes all things are seen as Buddha," means that the personality as an entity is not seen because all are seen as phenomena of no-self. When saying, eating, taking a shit, sleeping, and even having sex, there is only a phenomenon of action, not a doer as a being with volition. So are all thoughts; the truth is as it is.

A sin is not a bad action itself but the thought that "I did" the action. One is suffering because the ego always mistakenly identifies itself with a doer.

Although there arise various phenomena in the body-mind, they come from one. Likewise, all things and phenomena arising in the universe are one because they have no subjectivity.

The manifested world is full of pseudo-entities that are speaking with an air of importance. From the perspective of the enlightened one, what a comedy this world is!

No-self and true self are the same in meaning. However, the concept of no-self must be approached from the perspective of the seeker. There is a profound meaning to the term "no-self" that the Buddha used instead of the "true self" touted by Brahmanism, the mainstream at the time in India; he was considerate to human (ego) psychology. If approaching the truth as the true self or pan-self instead of no-self, one will instead create a vast ego. After enlightenment, one comes to know that it is not necessary to use such terms as true self, pan-self, no-self, but before that, one must proceed with no-self.

The enlightened one does not have no-mind but does not cling to it, does not have no-thought but is not attached to it. It is because there is not even the thought of this body-mind as 'I.'

Just as the wave of water is not newly created but manifested with a change of conditioning in the sea, the manifested world is not something created by true nature but only the phenomenon that true nature manifested itself into.

Do not try to make the body-mind become Buddha. They are illusory things; things arising must disappear. There is no truth in them. Only the perception that there is no-self in them is the truth.

If wanting to experience the fact that the body-mind is not "I," you must first understand but then do not cling to it. Then you will experience it naturally. If you have a deep experience of no-I in your heart, the body-mind can no longer bind true nature.

True nature is reality, absence of all conceptualizations; being of I-am-ness. All phenomena are just concepts: Buddha, enlightenment, nirvana are all only concepts that can exist as objects in the relative phenomenal world.

The enlightened one is not an individual personality anymore; only the presence of consciousness. If the body passes away, then consciousness also will disappear.

Because life proceeds by the prewritten script, eventually

what will be, will be, and what will not be, will not be. Suffering and bondage arise when one tries to block what will be, to wish what will not be, and regret what happened, feeling guilty.

Life is not reality but a play performed like the prewritten script of a dream. When perceiving that all objects are illusions, not personal subjects, one does not suffer, playing any role pleasantly without clinging and delivering responsibility.

Understanding in the mind is just conceptualization, not enlightenment. Enlightenment is a spontaneous perception through insight.

Because the enlightened one has no thought of the body-mind as oneself, they are always in a state of bliss and there is neither sacred nor vulgar.

If one just witnesses all phenomena arising in the body-mind without intervening or being affected, there begins to appear a gap between the body-mind and the ego identifying itself with the body-mind. If one keeps on watching, one comes to know that someday the ego falls away from the body-mind, which becomes nothing but a phenomenon and has no relation with true nature. That is enlightenment, a state of no-self.

The surface of the sea is sometimes calm or sometimes it has big waves arising on it. The unenlightened one will be affected according to the state of the surface, but the enlightened one will be in the calmness of the deep and thus will not be affected or bound by thought and action, regardless of the state of the surface—because there is not a self to be affected.

Someone claiming enlightenment might say that he completely rid himself of three poisons (desire, anger, ignorance) and never deludes himself. However, he is not the enlightened one because there must be an "I" who overcame three poisons and is not deluded. Now he believes that he has overcome the three poisons through his spiritual practice, but what shall he do if any of the three poisons returns? Will he give back his enlightenment? Then can we only evaluate ultimate enlightenment after death? Such ignorance is from misidentification with the psychosomatic apparatus, the body-mind complex, as self. Enlightenment is perfectness, never deluded once realized, regardless of the illusory thoughts and actions of the body.

The truth is very simple and clear to the enlightened. However, to the unenlightened it is like a cloud that they try to catch but cannot. Why is this? It is because they have to overturn all the concepts believed until now as the truth. Although they have overturned each false concept through spiritual practice, there is still a minute misidentification subtly functioning. If you can overturn false things easily, it is no problem. But it is not simple to do so, due to the fixed habits made by your ignorance.

Sexual desire is a survival instinct of all creatures. If seeing it from the perspective of an individual entity, one shall have endless suffering, yet if seeing it without dualistic discrimination, it will not differ from other phenomena appearing in the manifested world. All phenomena are temporal and cannot influence true nature.

Because good-evil, truth-falsehood exist relatively like two sides of a coin, if one side appears, the other side will disappear repeatedly. So long as there remains the ego of dualistic discrimination, it will be impossible to attain enlightenment and perceive the whole.

The best blessing for the seeker is to be directly taught by an enlightened master; next is to discover the teachings of the enlightened, and the last is to believe in and follow a religion, the shell of the enlightened. There is an enormous difference among the three.

Thinking about what we have to do or not is itself defilement and illusion. There is no independent personality that is able to decide to do something or not. All things are only a drama in a dream in which true nature manifests itself into hundreds of billions of phenomena. Because everything should be done by prewritten script, no volition can function. Although there arose some thought, word, or action, they cannot be defilements if there is no notion of "I did."

All the material things, thoughts, and actions manifested in the phenomenal world will disappear as objects if consciousness ceases. Therefore they cannot be reality. The reality is only that, true nature, which always exists whether consciousness functions or not.

Although the enlightened one might carry out a bad thought or action, there is nothing other than the truth to him; conversely, although the unenlightened might make a sacred and compassionate thought or action, for him there is nothing other than the false.

All beings in the phenomenal world are manifestations of true nature. Because there is no relative cognition in the truth, the creator and the created are not two separate things. All thoughts and actions proceed only along with the script written by true nature. The script is automatically written by dependent origination through mutual dependence. Who controls and discriminates except true nature? It is the truth as it is.

The fundamental question of the seeker is, "Who is seeking enlightenment?" So long as there remains someone seeking it, there is no possibility of it happening.

All thoughts, actions, and events arise by themselves; there is no "I" as an individual that has any volition to interfere with them and experience the effects. If there is one with responsibility for the cause-effect, it is only true nature, without the concept of an individual entity.

It is not a proper expression that, "there is Buddhahood in all matters of the phenomenal world"; this carries a nuance that there are other elements besides itself. All matters consist only of Buddhahood.

In a state of misidentifying oneself with this body-mind, one could not find the right path due to getting off on the wrong foot. It is the key to enlightenment to have the right view, that is, that there is no "I" as an independent self and that the body-mind is not "I."

How much merit and virtue was there for the lady who gave food to the Buddha? Nothing. Because there was no one who either gave or received it.

The middle way is the absoluteness by which both relative extremes cease, and so is a state of the Absolute, the nature of enlightenment, without dualistic discrimination against form or emptiness.

The urge to seek freedom is bondage. When this seeking ceases, freedom will appear by itself without any desire and obstacle.

If the mind goes into the inner side, it will stay in pure consciousness and the absolute truth will appear, whereas if it goes outside, it will stay in dualistic consciousness and the relative ego will come out.

Destiny is already set by the law of cause and effect. Therefore, if one attracts or expels the relationships coming and going, it is defilement and suffering. All existence is just a continuous process of appearing and disappearing, and so like-dislike also is only a temporary phenomenon of birth-death. If silently watching these relationships, one will see they arise and pass away along with dependent origination; why does one cling to them?

I am not in the universe but it is in me. That means that the phenomenal universe is in consciousness. Consciousness creates all things. However, mind is illusory, not existing. It is just a shadow of light from the true nature, reality. Therefore mind, body, self, spirit, and the manifested world are phenomena and thus delusions.

Just as a dewdrop on a blade of grass at dawn disappears when the sun rises, our body-mind and the seemingly permanent phenomenal universe will disappear when the curtain of ignorance blocking the light of truth is open.

If knowing how vivid and vast the dream dreamed by consciousness is, one would be surprised. Because of that, one could hardly believe it to be a dream. However, it is like a complicated epic drama; even though it is complicated, it should proceed in good order according to the script, the dependent origination.

Consciousness of presence, the first thought of it, is the first and last ego; this is alpha and omega, true nature, the being itself, Brahman, God-ness, Buddhahood. If arriving at this, then one has to give up the first thought. Then there remains only the Absolute, not to be named and of no beginning, no ending, because of its purity.

Buddha lives in pure consciousness and sentient beings live in the individual consciousness. Buddha realizes true nature to be always free from anything, whereas sentient beings suffer as they wander in a dream, an illusory life controlled by ego, identifying themselves with the body-mind.

The life that humans cling to is meaningless, like a word spoken or a thought arising and disappearing in a moment.

The manifesting process of the entire universe in consciousness is copied as it is into that of a small "universe" in the functioning of the body-mind; in the absence of consciousness in a deep sleep can nothing be cognized, but if consciousness stirs and a thought arises, a dreamed world will be created. The subject, as "I," is obviously consciousness dreaming, but identifies itself with someone in the dream and cognizes other objects apart from itself. Therefore, the same seven feelings and three poisons function in the dream as they do in the waking state. Upon waking, one comes to recognize that they were not real, just a dream. Therefore, the only way to cease suffering in a dream is to wake up.

Likewise the only way to cease suffering in an individual life—a waking dream—is to wake from the dream of life, to be enlightened.

Breathing occurs by itself although we do not plan or worry about when and how to breathe. Life does the same; life is to be lived despite there being no plan and no attention.

People call me friend, husband, father, son, brother, etc., but I am never truly those. However, because life itself follows a script, such roles can be acted without any problem. If actors do not perform their roles, the play will get into a mess. However, they are only acting and do not identify themselves with their roles. The one who acts the role of a robber has to perform the role with feeling. But if he thinks himself a robber, then there will be a problem. It is a fool who hates an actor because of a role that they didn't like in a play, because it is just a play. Enlightenment is to perceive the following facts: an individual life is that of an actor in the play written by true self, true nature, and the phenomenal universe that includes all beings, and humanity exists only in the play. Just as if it were a dream, it vanishes after waking.

When there arises sexual desire, one can be at a loss. It is a defilement that I think of myself as having sexual desire, but not a defilement to me that the feeling of desire happens.

The biggest obstacles to the seeker are money and sex. If one is not bound to money, one is free to use it, and it having sex does not matter if one is not bound to it. However, because someone may not be able to handle these things if not enlightened, one needs guardrails. After being enlightened, one does not need them anymore, because the individual self that requires such restraints simply disappears.

When the enlightened one says "I," it means true self, true nature; when the unenlightened one says "I," it means an individual self, and so they cannot communicate with each other; one talks of chalk, the other talks of cheese.

It is said that there are two paths to seek the truth: the way of wisdom and the way of devotion. However, with devotion it is easy to fall into blind belief and eventually wisdom will be needed to get out of it. Therefore there might be two paths in the beginning but they come to be one—wisdom—in the end.

To develop wisdom, one needs *samathi*; *samathi* without wisdom is like an ignorant sleep, whereas wisdom without *samathi* is just useless knowledge. The final door of wisdom and devotion is that "self" disappears.

Aspects of life after enlightenment are not the same. The Buddha traveled all around India to share his teachings with hundreds of thousands of disciples. Maharshi, on the other hand, met only people who came to his hermitage all his life. Like Maharaj, there are masters who do not leave home yet have taught all their life. Such various styles of teachings are manifestations of the true self and natural aspects of acting the roles given to each teacher.

The enlightened one has no-self. Therefore it is not that they will not be reborn, but that they were never born. And so there is no death. It is impossible to understand that conceptually. It is also impossible to get rid of the mind because the mind does not exist originally. It is instead necessary to remove the thought of the mind as "I."

Life is not bondage or suffering but people just think of it as such; in effect it is a play, often a comic one.

There exist only material and mental phenomena in the manifested world. However, there are no such things in true nature.

If the first thought, "I am," is the start of ego, the last one, "I am not," becomes nirvana. When moving beyond the mind to the heart, one becomes enlightened.

Enlightenment is not a long way off, or difficult to arrive at. One just cannot see the truth as true (ignorance) because each person wears their own colored glasses (ego). If realizing one's upside-down thoughts (wisdom) and taking off those glasses, one can see as it is; the true as true, the false as false. That is enlightenment.

If one sees the truth as true, practice itself is a foolish exercise. All things arising shall pass away by themselves. Therefore the thought of practice comes from ego; the desire to get out of a trap made by oneself. However, enlightenment cannot be attained by some desire of the ego. When desire is given up, the hidden true nature will come out.

Even if your eyes are open, if a thought is stopped, there is no universe. When a thought arises, the universe comes to exist. The body-mind, the entire manifested world are just illusions arising and vanishing in the consciousness. If a thought arises and then another, they will arise endlessly. Therefore the universe comes to exist endlessly when a thought arises. If you stop all thoughts and withdraw just one thought, everything that was is annihilated. Enlightenment is nothing more than withdrawing the thought, "I am." To do this, why does one need a long sitting practice, chakra practice, compassionate activity, praying, etc.? Those just inflate the ego. Later someone may have to claim that only when knowing the exact number of pores in the body or the total length of its blood vessels, will enlightenment occur. This is a joke, but a very serious one.

Most people cling to concepts and the truth is beyond them. They cannot see clear facts. The enlightened master uses the concepts to give them understanding, and some can later be led toward breaking past the concepts.

The thought of "I am" is the first ego and "mine" is the second. The second one is too broad. Generally the bigger the grouping, the bigger the ego. Thoughts of "mine" include religion, race, ideology, and humanity.

Although we describe someone who reaches enlightenment as "the entity becoming no-self," the expression is wrong; however, we have no choice but to use it due to the limits of language. Even the enlightened ones sleep and dream. But there is only the phenomenon of dreaming, not the subject of it. Even the enlightened eat and shit, but there is only the manifestation of these actions, not an individual doer with volition.

The enlightened one wants to be brought down to the level of sentient beings to teach them. However, when conveying the truth, he or she must be very stern about the perspective of the Absolute, in order to develop the intuitive power of the seeker without giving them room for reversed thought (ego).

There is too much intellectual knowledge, and it is a pity to try to get more into your mind. Someday a seeker will have to undergo hardship to be induced to throw away everything they thought they knew.

If the calm sea of the mind experiences a thought, waves appear on the surface, but the waves cannot exist for long before they have to go back to the original calm again. Thus all beings in the phenomenal world are manifestations of a thought in the consciousness. However, just as a wave is a wave as it is, all beings are being itself and have aspects of manifestations of life without "me and you." They appear for a moment, but in the end go back to their calm source.

The five fingers look different from each other but are connected as one—they cannot be separated. Thus all beings in the phenomenal world look different, but cannot be separated into independent entities.

The religious who worship the Buddha, Jesus or various other beings as sacred never can be enlightened, because they always see themselves as different from the object of their worship.

Because the dream, the phenomenal world, is a dream of universal consciousness, it is cognized as the same by me and you. However, an individual dreamer experiences different situations. Nevertheless, the subjectivity of all things is only one consciousness; not to be separated whether it is universal or individual.

A state of deep sleep is a rest for the consciousness and so there is no feeling of conscious presence. A state of true nature is one of no discrimination that a feeling of conscious presence exists or not.

Three poisons(greed, anger, ignorance) arise when the mind looks outwards; precept, *samathi*, and insight are the means to refocus the mind inward. However, the means is not the purpose. Once the purpose is achieved, then one should throw away the means. If the means is still needed, it is proof that one has not yet reached the goal.

It is true practice when one goes into one's inner side regardless of the waves of the sea, and stays in pure consciousness witnessing it as it is, not trying to make the waves on the sea calm.

The seeker has to accept all people and the entire phenomenal world as a teacher. You should know that the one who gave you the worst mental and physical suffering is your greatest teacher, because they let you realize that life is suffering and led you to the truth. An ego usually loves the one who gives pleasure, but hates the one who gives suffering. When the feeling of love and hate approach being equal, you come close to enlightenment.

Because all beings stay in time and space just as concepts, there is endless dispute on the concepts of creation, evolution, life-death, etc. The concept of time and space exists as a circle, not on a plane or linear flow.

Just as you identify something with reality in a dream, you can cognize it as a dream not reality when waking. You come to know that if you bring back the consciousness to the inner side so that it stays with the true self even in a state of waking, the reality cognized by the five senses does not really exist, but is just a dream.

The absolute nature yet unmanifested is before alpha and after omega, whereas the consciousness manifested is alpha and omega. Each shape that continuously arises and passes away is a state of no-self, having no volitional existence.

All thoughts and actions are true as they are but if intervened with or attached to they are defilements and delusions.

Ignorance is like an onion, with more layers appearing as you peel the outer ones away. Before realizing the emptiness of the inner side by oneself, one cannot understand that there is inherently no-self in the nature of all beings.

So long as one identifies the manifested world with reality and oneself with an independent personality, one cannot be free from bondage and suffering.

One day Zuangzhi became a butterfly flying around flowers in a dream and woke up. Waking from the dream, Zuangzhi said, "I do not know whether Zuangzhi became a butterfly in a dream or a butterfly became Zuangzhi in a dream." There is a deep philosophy in that saying; one can be a being and live some kind of life, but at the moment of waking up one knows that it was a kind of delusion. He is metaphorically and figuratively saying that even the reality awakened into from a dream of being a butterfly is in effect just a dream.

The Way (Tao) is not mysticism. Most people generally think that the Way is somehow mystical and fantastic, that it must be a different dimension from the world. Therefore the term 'master of the Way' came to refer to the one who can freely perform miracles, and so there are many seekers who do not know the right path of the Way and are misled with delusion. Essentially, without the ability to judge what is true or not, it is no more than trickery. People wish to acquire supernatural powers to see far away, read minds, know the future, etc., through practices like Danjeon breathing or Qi-gong.

There is a self, however, an ego, in such wishes and in all such phenomena. Therefore, to maximize the ego and "complete" the self is not the right path. The self, an individual entity, cannot be completed no matter how one tries, because the entity is intrinsically a delusion and the body-mind consists of material things. The body-mind that appears according to the conditions of earth, water, fire, and air stays on the time-space of the phenomenal world and in due time returns to the same conditions. Then what is the true Way? It is not to dream something illusory but only to realize no-self and be one with true nature through recognizing ego as a delusion. Any other supernatural power or spiritual experience will not be the essence of the Way. Such things are just phenomena caused by the ego appearing during practice. If you cling to an individual self, you come to lose the Way, because the ego is at the center of such supernatural powers. When one is captivated by such things, in the end the ego becomes stronger and one strays far from the Way. It is a pity that nowadays so many seekers are unknowingly going hard along such a wrong path.

The Way is not mysticism. It is just as it is; it is the true nature to be in a state of one hundred percent purity, not tainted by even a particle of ego. This state is possible only when not thinking of this body-mind as oneself. Therefore the enlightened masters said, "The true self does not come and go," in order to show the true nature of the Way. The true Way is to realize that intrinsically I am the Absolute through being no-self, a state of nirvana, without the ego of attachment and dualistic discrimination by realizing that an ego, an individual mind, is just a delusion.

There is a gradation in the ignorance and attachment of sentient beings. Some cling only to the seen body and material things, and do anything to get money, fame, or power. Those who are interested in spirituality think that the body and material possessions are illusions and not permanent, and believe that the spirit will exist forever, clinging to the non-physical spiritual world. Someone who is in this state understands that the source of all manifestations is void, but does not get rid of the ego completely. Only when realizing no-self in the heart, free from dualistic discrimination and staying on the middle path as it is, does one become truly enlightened.

The enlightened one is not a person who does not have attachment, desire, and dualistic discrimination. There is not a self who causes such attachment, desire, etc. in him: there is no-self.

To explain fundamental ignorance, it is often quoted that a person sometimes mistakes a rope for a snake when walking on the road at night and runs away. The reason for being afraid is that they saw a snake, but the fear is needless, as it was a rope.

Then what is really wrong? It is that they did not see correctly and mistook the rope for a snake. Likewise, because they mistakenly identify themselves with the body-mind, people are in suffering and fear. Vipassana meditation is one of the practices that can be used to check the body-mind thoroughly. If suffering because you are identifying the true self with the false self, should you not verify the facts and free yourself from the fear and suffering as soon as possible?

It is in the aspects of the phenomenal universe that the true nature manifests itself into innumerable forms. They are originally one and cannot be divided forever. However, the dualistic consciousness of humans divides all things. All the material things and events are truth as they are, but nevertheless dualistic discrimination makes true nature contaminated.

One day Gongzhi went to Laozhi. But Gongzhi was expelled from the gate with an angry scolding by Laozhi, because Gongzhi confused people with humanity and justice. It might be a story forged by Taoism, but it is true. All philosophers, thinkers, and religious leaders in the world are the same in this respect; they develop such useless things to make people confused. Now humanity has to throw away all the garbage from their heads and hearts so that they can get back to true nature. Then if there comes a state of no-self without dualistic discrimination, the truth will appear as it is.

When there is cognition of *I*, the others all become *you*. If there is not a thought of *I*, the object of *you* will disappear to be one with the whole. Therefore if there is not an ego, *I*, the entire manifested universe becomes *I*. However, because the phenomenal world consists of changing materials, it is not the truth. A state of permanence is the true nature of the fundamental source of the truth.

The understanding of this merely as knowledge is not enlightenment. Enlightenment is pure consciousness free from dualistic discrimination after the ego disappears. And it is the enlightened one who reaches such a state.

When the true self as true nature is compared to a screen of no-mind, all aspects of life played on the screen are compared to the physical phenomenal world, and consciousness is witnessing the movie. While watching the movie, one can mistakenly identify the scenes on screen with real existences and feel all sorts of emotions. After the movie ends, all images on the screen disappear and only the screen of no-mind remains; the screen exists as the original, untainted by the images that were played on it. The consciousness of the enlightened is never tainted by life while living a life, because they perceive that a life is just an illusion of appearing-disappearing. The body-mind, the false self, is born to disappear.

Across all ages and countries, it is very rare that the enlightened one is recognized by their family, friends, or neighbors. This is because they have seen the person as an image, one that was never different from them, or perhaps even inferior to them in terms of human ability. Further, they might think that the enlightened person is supposed to demonstrate supernatural powers, and when they do not it is rather easy to treat them as insane.

However, something extraordinary happened in India 2500 years ago. The ones whom the Buddha, Sakyamuni, had first called on after enlightenment were the five fellow seekers who had left him, condemning his giving up asceticism. They did not say anything when Sakyamuni visited them at first, but they eventually accepted his enlightenment in earnest and all became his first disciples.

The Song of Enlightenment

The Sun Has No Shadow

The sun has not its own shadow

The sun shines on everything

casting shadows,

whereas, nothing can shine on it

Even the sun cannot shine on itself

because it is the light itself

As It Comes

A rolling stone, as it comes

a speck of cloud floating

a bird singing

a stream flowing as in a dream

Mountains and streams are as they are,

whereas, the witness has changed

Even no birth and no death,

then no comings and no goings

The Way It Is

All being as it is

wind blowing as it is

clouds floating as it is

water flowing as it is

flowers blooming as it is

leaves falling as it is

All appearing and disappearing, as it is

As You Are

Be happy when happy

be sad when sad

love when loving

be awake when awake

be alive when alive

Originally No-Self

There is no thinker, only thinking

There is no talker, only talking

There is no doer, only doing

Originally the Absolute

From the relative phenomenal point of view,

There, me and you

From the Absolute whole point of view,

There, originally one

In the phenomenal world,

There, continuously appearing and disappearing

Whereas, even if appearing,

There, oneness

Even if disappearing,

There, oneness

By Itself

All thoughts, words and actions arising

in the body-mind

not done by "I"

Life is lived by itself,

not by an entity of its own volition

Seekers of the Way

Some people are seeking the Way

In mountains, fields, and villages

there, lonely ones wandering away

for seeking the truth

People do not know

that the truth is as it is

Sea and Waves

A vast number of waves rising

on the calm sea by the wind

But there only the sea of waves,

no such waves

Enlightenment

Though the enlightenment came over,

there is nothing to be changed

Only disappeared the ignorance

of misidentifying with this body-mind

Now the play of individual entity is over,

only the appearing of the Absolute

The Man of Great Freedom

The great freeman

has no duality of you and me

has no discrimination of right and wrong

has no delusions in the ever-changing world of life

Everything in the world

is like a bubble rising and falling in a moment

without any trace in mind

There is no coming and going

no tracks of steps

no bondage at all

like water, wind, and cloud

That is the man of great freedom

Transcendence

There is no-I, therefore,

when thinking, not in the thought

when talking, not in the talk

when acting, not in the act

when fighting, not in the fight

when happy, not in the happiness

when sad, not in the sadness

when loving, not in the love

when living, not in the life

when dying, not in the death

Glossary

Amita Buddha

A celestial Buddha described in the scriptures of the Mahāyāna school of Buddhism; the principal Buddha in the Pure Land sect, a branch of Buddhism practiced mainly in East Asia. In Vajrayana Amitābha he is known for his longevity, magnetizing the red fire element, the aggregate of discernment, pure perception, and the deep awareness of the uniqueness of phenomena.

Arhat

In Theravada Buddhism, an *Arhat* (Sanskrit: *arhat*; Pali: *arahant*; "one who is worthy") is a "perfected person" who has attained nirvana. In other Buddhist traditions the term has also been used for people far advanced along the path of enlightenment, the personal ideal of Theravada Buddhism.

Bodhi

Bodhi (Sanskrit) in Buddhism is the understanding pos-

243

sessed by a Buddha regarding the true nature of things. It is traditionally translated into English with the word enlightenment and literally means "awakened." (The verbal root "budh" means to awaken.) Bodhi is knowledge of the causal mechanism by which beings incarnate into material form and experience suffering. Although its most common usage is in the context of Buddhism, Bodhi is also present as a concept in other Indian philosophies and traditions.

Bodhisattva

In Buddhism, an enlightened (*bodhi*) being (*sattva*). Traditionally, a bodhisattva is anyone who, motivated by great compassion, has generated *bodhicitta*, which is a spontaneous wish to attain Buddhahood for the benefit of all sentient beings. According to Tibetan Buddhism, a bodhisattva is one of the four sublime states a human can achieve in life (the others being an arhat, Buddha, or pratyekabuddha

Dan-jeon breathing

Practicing through a prescribed set of slow-moving exercises accompanied by controlled, forceful deep breathing. Each breath is drawn in through the nose and expelled through the mouth. You should try to expand your abdomen rather than your chest.

Dharma

The transcendent substratum of single elements of conscious life; a part of conscious life; the subject of Buddhist teachings; the teachings or religion of Buddha; appearance, truth, law, ordinance; that which sustains a firm code of conduct and duty. In a metaphysical sense Dharma means the laws of Nature that sustain the operation of the universe, the inherent properties of elements, for example the Dharma of fire is to burn. Another meaning is the name of Bodhidaharma, the first patriarch of the Chinese Chan.

Gong

Sunya in Sanskrit: emptiness; non-substantial matters; no-self, no form, non-existence, unmanifested

Hega (Huike)

Dazu Huike (487–593) is considered the Second Patriarch of Chinese Chán and the twenty-ninth since Gautama Buddha. A scholar in both Buddhist scriptures and classical Chinese texts, including Taoism, Huike was considered enlightened but criticized for not having a teacher. He met his teacher Bodhidharma at the Shaolin Monastery in 528 when he was about forty years old and studied with Bodhidharma for six years (although some sources say four years, five years, or nine years).

Hua-tou

Koan or Gongan; the patterns of zen school that use the accounts of Zen masters; doubtable questions to lead zen practice. In the past, patriarchal monks of China and Korea were enlightened through investigating Hua-tou.

Karma

Action, especially responsible action; good and evil; the principle of causality, popularly known as the law of cause and effect. Karma is closely associated with the idea of rebirth in some schools of Asian religions. In these schools, karma in the present affects one's future in the current life, as well as the nature and quality of future lives—or, one's *saṃsāra*.

Ki-Practice

Qigong: Practice of aligning body, breath, and mind for health, meditation, and martial-arts training; traditionally viewed as a practice to cultivate and balance ki (qi) or what has been translated as "life energy."

Kstigarbha Bodhisattva

A bodhisattva primarily revered in East Asian Buddhism and usually depicted as a Buddhist monk. His name may be translated as 'Earth Treasury,' 'Earth Store,' 'Earth Matrix,' or 'Earth Womb.' Ksitigarbha is known for his vow to take responsibility for the instruction of all beings in the six worlds between the death of Gautama Buddha and the rise of Maitreya, as well as his vow not to achieve Buddhahood until all hells are emptied. He is therefore often regarded as the bodhisattva of hell-beings, as well as the guardian of children and patron deity of deceased children and aborted fetuses in Japanese culture.

Laozi

A philosopher and poet of ancient China. He is best known as the reputed author of the *Tao Te Ching* and the founder of philosophical Taoism, but he is also revered as a deity in religious Taoism and traditional Chinese religions. Although a legendary figure, he is usually dated to around the 6th century BC and reckoned a contemporary of Confucius, but some historians contend that he actually lived during the Warring States period of the 5th or 4th century BC.[3] A central figure in Chinese culture, Laozi is claimed by both the emperors of the Tang dynasty and modern people of the Li surname as a founder of their lineage. Throughout history, Laozi's work has been embraced by various anti-authoritarian movements.

Mahayana

Literally the 'Great Vehicle': one of two (or three, under some classifications) main existing branches of Buddhism and a term for classification of Buddhist philosophies and practice; referring to the path of the bodhisattva seeking complete enlightenment for the benefit of all sentient beings.

Mantra

Instrument of thought; hymn, incantation. Ideal sounds visualized as letters and vocalized as syllables. Constant repetition of mantra produces the desired specific results by unfolding latent psychic and occult faculties.

Means

Upaya (Sanskrit): Expediency suitable to the condition, circumstantial method, and method of education that is used for people who have no capability to understand. Provisional practice to enter the right path.

Mugeuk

Opposite to Taegeuk, limitlessness, Absoluteness, emptiness, boundlessness. Taeguk comes from Mugeuk.

Mu-Wi

Wu wei (Chinese, meaning 'non-doing') is an important concept in Taoism that literally means 'non-action.' In the *Tao te Ching*, Laozi explains that beings (or phenomena) that are wholly in harmony with the Tao behave in a completely natural, uncontrived way. The goal of spiritual practice for the human being is, according to Laozi, the attainment of this purely natural way of behaving, as when the planets revolve around the sun. The planets do this revolving without any sort of control, force, or attempt to revolve themselves, instead engaging in effortless and spontaneous movement.

Nagarjuna

Chinese: *Lóngshù (Ryūju)*; 150–250 CE; widely considered one of the most important Buddhist philosophers after Gautama Buddha. Along with his disciple Āryadeva, he is considered to be the founder of the Madhyamaka school of

Mahāyāna Buddhism. Nāgārjuna is also credited with developing the philosophy of the Prajñāpāramitā sūtras and, in some sources, with having revealed these scriptures to the world, having recovered them from the *nāgas* (snake-people). Furthermore, he is traditionally supposed to have written several treatises on *rasayana* as well as serving a term as the head of Nālandā, a renowned Buddhist university.

Nikaya

A term from the Sanskrit and Pali language meaning "group."

Nisargadatta Maharaj

He was born in Mumbai in 1896. He worked on a farm as a boy and grew up with little or no formal education. He was exposed to religious ideas by his father's friend, a pious Brahman. When he was 34, a friend of his introduced him to his guru, Sri Siddharameshwar Maharaj. The guru gave a mantra and some instructions to him. This self-realized master become famous for brilliant, aphoristic, extemporized talks in which he taught an austere, minimalist Jnana Yoga based on his own experience. Many of these talks have been published in books. The earliest volume, *I Am That*, is widely regarded as a modern classic.

Osho Rajneesh

(December 11, 1931–January 19, 1990), also known as Acharya Rajneesh from the 1960s onwards, as Bhagwan Shree during the 1970s and 1980s, and as Osho from 1989, was an Indian mystic, guru, and spiritual teacher. His international following has continued beyond his death. A professor of philosophy, he traveled throughout India during the 1960s as a public speaker. His outspoken criticism of politicians and the political mind, Mahatma Gandhi, and institutionalized religion made him controversial. He advocated a more open attitude towards sexuality, a stance which earned him the sobriquet of 'sex guru' in the Indian and (later) international press. In 1970 Rajneesh settled for a time in Bombay, initiating disciples (known as neo-sannyasins) and assuming the role of spiritual teacher. In his discourses he reinterpreted the writings of religious traditions, mystics, and philosophers from around the world.

Pure Land

Pure Land oriented practices and concepts are found within basic Mahāyāna Buddhist cosmology, and form an important component of the Mahāyāna Buddhist traditions of China, Japan, Korea, Vietnam, and Tibet. Contemporary Pure Land traditions see Amitābha expounding the Dharma in his Buddha-field , or 'pure land' (Chinese, *jìngtǔ*), a region offering respite from karmic transmigration. Amitābha's pure land is described as a land of beauty that surpasses all other realms. It is said to be inhabited by many gods, men, flowers, fruits, and to be adorned with wish-granting trees where rare birds come to rest.

Ramana Maharshi

Ramana Maharshi (December 30, 1879–April 14, 1950) is widely acknowledged as one of the outstanding Hindu gurus of modern times. He was born Venkataraman Iyer, in Tiruchuli, Tamil Nadu, South India, and given the name Bhagavan Sri Ramana Maharshi in 1907 by one of his first devotees, Ganapati Muni. This would be the name by which he became known to the world. At the age of sixteen, Venkataraman lost his sense of individual selfhood, an awakening which he later recognized as enlightenment. Six weeks later he left his home to journey to the holy mountain Arunachala, Tiruvannamalai, where he remained for the rest of his life.

Saek

Rupa in Sanskrit; form, one of the five accumulations: outward appearance, manifested; it has resistance or changes and disappears as a part of the five sensual objects or the five origins; the object of the eyes which is color or substance.

Samadhi

Superconscious state, profound meditation (*sam*, together + *a*, to + *dhi*, placing; putting together). Samadhi is a yogic practice in which the seeker becomes one with his object of meditation, thus attaining unqualified bliss. Concentrating the discomposed mind in order to free it from delusional defilements; keeping the mind in the stage of tranquility which is an equal stage of contemplation.

Samsara

Reincarnation, rebirth, turning around like a wheel of a wagon. The round of existence, samsara is the passage of the soul in the cycle of birth and death.

Sati

Sati (in Pali), translated as mindfulness or awareness, is a spiritual or psychological faculty (*indriya*) that forms an essential part of Buddhist practice. It refers to either not forgetting one's practice instructions, or not forgetting to keep the mind focussed on and not distracted from instructions or vows etc.

Sayadaw

A Myanmar Theravada Buddhist title used to refer to the senior monk of a temple. Famous sayadaws would often be referred to as a sayadawgyi. The words "sayadaw" and "sayadawgyi" originally meant the monks who taught the Myanmar kings. Sayadaws are the main teachers of Buddhism and are also meditation practitioners.

Seo Jeong-ju

He is considered one of the best poets in 20th-century Korean literature, writing under the pen name Midang. He was born in 1915 in what is now South Korea. His poems are seen as having a subservient attitude towards the Japanese and the dictators who ruled Korea after Liberation. His work is also modernistic and surrealistic, being influenced by foreign literature.

Seon-do

A holistic self-development practice system aiming to develop the ultimate physical strength, the ultimate mental power, and the ultimate spiritual enlightenment. A deep abdominal energy center breathing known as Dan-jeon breathing that enables the practitioners to breathe the universal life energy, qi, into the body.

Taegeuk

The ultimate reality from which all things and values are derived. It helps to understand that *taegeuk* is the Korean pronunciation of the Chinese ideograms often translated as 'Grand Ultimate,' although literally meaning 'great polarity,' and when taken together, are commonly associated with Taoist philosophical values as well as indigenous Korean Sinism.

The Way (Tao)

A Chinese concept signifying 'way,' 'path,' 'route,' or sometimes more loosely 'doctrine' or 'principle.' Within the context of traditional Chinese philosophy and religion, the Tao is the understanding or intuitive knowing of 'life,' or present awareness, that cannot be grasped full-heartedly as just a concept but is known nonetheless. Complete wisdom that comes from the enlightenment of four noble truths.

Theravada

A branch of Buddhism that uses the teaching of the Pali Canon, a collection of the oldest recorded Buddhist texts, as its doctrinal core, but also includes a rich diversity of traditions and practices that have developed over its long history of interactions with various cultures and communities. It is the dominant form of religion in Cambodia, Laos, Sri Lanka, Thailand, and Burma, and is practiced by minority groups in Vietnam, Bangladesh, and China. In addition, the diaspora of all of these groups as well as converts around the world practice Theravāda Buddhism.

Tripitaka Koreana

A large collection of Buddha's teachings that were recorded after Buddha's passing away. It is composed of the Vinaya, Sutra, and Abhidhamma. These form the foundation for the most important Buddhist scripture. Haeinsa Temple in Korea is the home of the Tripitaka Koreana.

Veda

A large body of texts originating in ancient India. Composed in Vedic Sanskrit, the texts constitute the oldest layer of Sanskrit literature and the oldest scriptures of Hinduism.

Yin-yang

Concepts used to describe how apparently opposite or contrary forces are actually complementary, interconnected, and interdependent in the natural world, and how they give rise to each other as they interrelate. Many tangible dualities (such as light and dark, fire and water, and male and female) are thought of as physical manifestations of the duality of yin and yang.

Yoga

A method by which consciousness is disconnected from the entanglement with mind and the manifested world. It is a unique psychiatric-psychological system leading to enlightenment and liberation. An adept in Yoga is called a Yogi.

Zhuangzi

Master Zhuang (late 4th century BC) is the pivotal figure in philosophical Taoism. This period in China was marked by humanist and natural reflections on normativity shaped by the metaphor of Tao (a social or a natural path). Traditional orthodoxy understood Zhuangzi as an anti-rational, credulous follower of a mystical Laozi.

About the Author

Muwi Haegong was born in 1958 in Seoul, Korea.

He became a Christian at fourteen years old, and took a vow to become a priest after having a spiritual experience at fifteen years old. After graduating from theological college, he began to serve the ministry in church. But later he left Christianity to become a seeker of truth.

After twenty years of practicing religions and philosophies from the East and West, he realized 'no-self,' transcending the individual ego, at the Mahashi Meditation Center in Myanmar in December 1998, bringing the seeker's long journey to an end.

He is now teaching truth and Vipassana meditation at the Haegong meditation center on Jeju Island.

www.ingramcontent.com/pod-product-compliance
Lightning Source LLC
Chambersburg PA
CBHW030148100526
44592CB00009B/169